Second Edition

Greenman and the Magic Forest

Contents

Teacher's Book A

Katie Hill & Karen Elliott

Shaftesbury Road, Cambridge CB2 8EA, United Kingdom

One Liberty Plaza, 20th Floor, New York, NY 10006, USA

477 Williamstown Road, Port Melbourne, VIC 3207, Australia

314–321, 3rd Floor, Plot 3, Splendor Forum, Jasola District Centre, New Delhi – 110025, India

103 Penang Road, #05–06/07, Visioncrest Commercial, Singapore 238467

José Abascal 56 –1º, 28003 Madrid, Spain

Cambridge University Press & Assessment is a department of the University of Cambridge.

We share the University's mission to contribute to society through the pursuit of education, learning and research at the highest international levels of excellence.

www.cambridge.org
Information on this title: www.cambridge.org/9781009219594

© Cambridge University Press & Assessment 2015, 2023

This publication is in copyright. Subject to statutory exception and to the provisions of relevant collective licensing agreements, no reproduction of any part may take place without the written permission of Cambridge University Press & Assessment.

First published 2015
Second edition 2023

20 19 18 17 16 15 14 13 12 11 10 9 8 7 6 5 4 3 2 1

Printed in Spain by Pulmen

A catalogue record for this publication is available from the British Library

ISBN	978-10-0921-959-4	Teacher's Book with Teacher's Digital Pack
ISBN	978-10-0921-939-6	Pupil's Book with Pupil's Digital Pack
ISBN	978-10-0921-967-9	Activity Book
ISBN	978-10-0921-968-6	Teacher's Book Castellano with Teacher's Digital Pack
ISBN	978-10-0921-970-9	Big Book
ISBN	978-10-0921-969-3	Flashcards
ISBN	978-10-0921-960-0	Classroom Presentation Software
ISBN	978-10-0921-958-7	Pupil's Online Resources
ISBN	978-10-0921-942-6	Home Practice E-book
ISBN	978-10-0921-948-8	Puppet

Cambridge University Press & Assessment has no responsibility for the persistence or accuracy of URLs for external or third-party Internet websites referred to in this publication and does not guarantee that any content on such websites is, or will remain, accurate or appropriate.

Acknowledgements

The authors and publishers acknowledge the following sources of copyright material and are grateful for the permissions granted. While every effort has been made, it has not always been possible to identify the sources of all the material used, or to trace all copyright holders. If any omissions are brought to our notice, we will be happy to include the appropriate acknowledgements on reprinting and in the next update to the digital edition, as applicable.

Key: U = Unit.

Photography

The following photographs have been sourced from Getty Images.
U2: Mint Images/Mint Images RF; Samart Boonyang/EyeEm; amtitus/DigitalVision Vectors; ViewStock; U6: andresr/E+; aleksandarvelasevic/DigitalVision Vectors; Summer: Jose Luis Pelaez Inc/DigitalVision; mikimad/DigitalVision Vectors

The following photographs have been sourced from other libraries:
U4: Pavel L Photo and Video/Shutterstock; U6: Michalakis Ppalis/Shutterstock.

Cover photography

Vreemous/DigitalVision Vectors

Illustration

Gema García Ingelmo: cover illustration and characters concept; Rosanna Crespo Picó: illustration

Audio

Audio production by Fernando J. Navarro Peral.

Typesetting

Aphik, S.A. de C.V.

Syllabus

Unit	Language	Phonics
Routines	**weather:** *cloudy, cold, hot, raining/rainy, snowing/snowy, sunny, windy* **shapes:** *circle, rectangle, square, triangle* **numbers:** *1–6* **colours:** *black, blue, brown, green, grey, orange, pink, purple, red, white, yellow*	
Welcome Unit: Let's be friends!	*Greenman, Nico, Sam; Hello, I'm (Sam). What's your name?; colours; family; toys* **numbers:** *1–4*	
Unit 1: Four rabbits	*bag, board, computer, door, peg, window; There are (three rabbits). There aren't (four rabbits).* **concepts:** *good/naughty* **emotions:** *being sorry* **value:** *being respectful*	a (ant) + e (egg)
Unit 2: The honey game	*sandpit, seesaw, slide, swing; bucket, spade; Let's play on the (swing). Where's (the seesaw)?* **concepts:** *up/down* **emotions:** *feeling happy* **value:** *exercising*	i (in) + o (on)
Review 1: Autumn fun!	*brown; leaves* **review:** *red, yellow; cloudy, cold, rainy, windy; classroom and playground vocabulary*	
Unit 3: I'm hurt!	*arm, finger, foot, hand, leg, tummy; What's the matter? My (leg) hurts.* **concepts:** *clean/dirty* **colours:** *black, brown, white* **numbers:** *5* **emotions:** *being hurt* **value:** *being careful*	l (leg)
Unit 4: It's too small!	*boots, coat, dress, hat, jumper, trousers; The/Your (dress) is/are too (small). Put on your (boots). Take off your (jumper).* **concepts:** *big/small* **colours:** *pink, purple* **emotions:** *feeling cold* **value:** *recycling*	oo (cook, moon)
Review 2: Winter fun!	*snowman* **review:** *white; cold, rainy, snowy, windy; body and clothes vocabulary*	
Unit 5: Can I help you?	*cow, hen, horse, pig, rabbit, sheep; eat, fly, jump, run, sleep, walk; Have you got (strong wings)? Yes, I have. No, I haven't. Can you (fly)? Yes, I can. No, I can't.* **concepts:** *strong/weak* **colours:** *grey, orange* **numbers:** *6* **emotions:** *feeling sad* **value:** *having self-confidence*	sh (sheep) + ee (bee)
Unit 6: The summer party	*carrot, egg, juice, plum, potato, sausage; Have you got any (eggs)? Can I have some (eggs)? Here you are. I like sharing my (eggs).* **concepts:** *hungry/thirsty* **emotions:** *being sorry* **value:** *sharing*	x (fox) + ng (sing)
Review 3: Spring fun!	**review:** *green, pink; flower; rainy, sunny, windy; animals and food vocabulary*	
World Peace Day	*dove, peace, world*	w (world)
World Book Day	*character, page, story book*	y (yellow) + oa (boat)
World Friendship Day	*be kind, play games, share*	ch (chair)
Green Day	*help, park, rubbish*	ai/ay (rainy day)
Review 4: Summer fun!	*beach, cool, holiday, swim* **review:** *blue, orange, yellow; hot, sunny; play course vocabulary*	

Welcome to *Greenman and the Magic Forest* Second Edition!

Magical adventures in early learning

It's a beautiful day in the magic forest. Three friends are on an adventure, singing songs and learning about the natural world. Let's explore together with Nico, Sam and our guide Greenman, the protector of the forest.

Greenman and the Magic Forest nurtures children as they grow and learn a new language, by helping to develop confident social interactions and a caring approach to nature.

Meet the characters

Hi, everyone! I'm Greenman, the protector of the magic forest. I take care of the forest and my friends who live and play here. And I really love honey! I'll take your children on a magical learning adventure.

Hi! We're Sam and Nico. We love to play with our friends in the magic forest. Your children can have fun learning English with us. We'll also show them how to look after the environment, enjoy nature and be healthy!

Hi! I'm Stella. I'm a Phonics snake, but I'm very friendly! Your children will practise sounds and letters with me.

Objectives

Greenman, Sam, Nico, Stella and their other forest friends introduce children to a delightful English-speaking world through stories and songs. Activities focus on developing independence, fine and gross motor skills, communication skills and social and emotional skills. The integrated curriculum encourages pupils to make connections to concepts they are learning in other subject areas, so that they study English as a means of learning about the world around them.

Methodology

This pre-primary period is one of the most important times for learning in a child's life. *Greenman and the Magic Forest* provides a unique, varied and enjoyable first English experience by stimulating young children's natural curiosity and desire to learn.

Greenman and the Magic Forest follows a holistic approach, teaching English as part of the children's overall learning and development. The lesson structure lends itself naturally to English acquisition. It features:

- a unique topic and story for each unit, with a unit value and emotion (such as 'recycling' and 'being sorry'), contrasting concepts (such as 'clean' and 'dirty') and relevant vocabulary to enhance all themes;
- six new key vocabulary words, presented in Lesson 1 of each unit;
- continuous recycling of language throughout the course to aid retention and comprehension;
- a wide variety of activities to spark pupils' enthusiasm and give opportunities for each child to feel a sense of achievement;
- songs that pupils will enjoy singing along with, while doing the TPR (Total Physical Response) actions they have learnt in class.

Pupils will get to know classroom routines in English with Greenman's help. Routines, stories, songs and games give pupils regular exposure to language, enabling them to learn and retain it while having fun. The connections made to values and emotions also help pupils to build on information that they have already had exposure to in their native language.

Since publication, we have asked teachers what they and their pupils love about the course, and how to make it even better.

What have we kept?

The things teachers and learners love:

- relatable **characters** who enjoy adventures in the natural world;
- strong **routines**, using seasons and nature as central themes;
- **stories** to blend the forest world with recognisable, 'real life' settings that pupils can relate to;
- fun and catchy **songs** and **raps** which use TPR movements to teach vocabulary in a style that pupils will enjoy and remember;
- special **phonics songs** to introduce new sounds;
- **story** and **action song videos**;
- age-appropriate **projects** which present the use of English in real situations.

What have we improved?

New design

- an exciting, fresh **page design** across all components to make activities even more engaging for young learners;
- redesigned activities to better suit the **fine motor skill development** of each specific age group;
- **Greenman Puppet** with a new improved design.

New content for the second edition

- a new **Forest Fun Activity Book** which promotes creativity and well-being and provides craft ideas and opportunities for cross-curricular learning;
- New **audio-visual** material, including vocabulary song videos, unit introduction videos and yoga videos.

Enhanced digital support

- **Presentation Plus** gives teachers easy access to resources in the classroom, including digital versions of the print components, and interactive activities that correspond to activities in the Pupil's Book;
- an innovative **Pupil's Digital Pack** on Cambridge One, your new home for digital learning, gives pupils access to all the course videos and songs in a simple format to make it even easier for children to practise English at home.

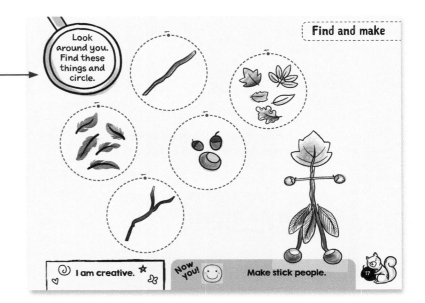

Components overview

For teachers

- The **Teacher's Book**, in full colour, includes information to help teachers plan and execute lessons. There is a full guide for each lesson, including optional activities and games for extension. The spiral binding makes the Teacher's Book easy to use while planning and teaching.

- The **Big Book**, with its full-colour illustrations of fun characters and lively action scenes, is an attractive component for young children. The Big Book includes six stories, which act as the main focus for each of the six main Pupil's Book units.

- **Flashcards** are ideal for this age group and provide pupils with a visual link to the vocabulary they hear and say in English. There are flashcards for the six new key vocabulary words in each unit.

- Lovable Greenman is a cuddly **puppet** which pupils will associate with English learning time in school. Since Greenman only speaks English, pupils are encouraged to stretch and improve their language skills, because they will want to make that effort to communicate with him.

- The enhanced **Teacher's Digital Pack** includes:

  » new Presentation Plus classroom software, which provides digital versions of the books and answer keys, interactive activities and games and interactive Routine Boards for reviewing colours, shapes and weather;
  » online materials including: Extra Festivals lessons, Phonics Flashcards, Letters to parents, Teacher Resources Worksheets and Class Audio and Video.

For pupils

- The **Pupil's Book** includes colour pages, as well as stickers and pop-outs. The wide format and spiral binding are easy for young children to manage as they learn to find page numbers, turn pages and complete activities within the book. The book includes tear-off worksheets, so the teacher has the option of sending home individual worksheets as homework.

- The new **Forest Fun Activity Book** supports themes from the Pupil's Book, such as caring for and enjoying the environment.

- New for the second edition, the **Pupil's Digital Pack** includes the new Home Practice material, which gives pupils access to all songs and videos from the course to sing along to and watch at home.

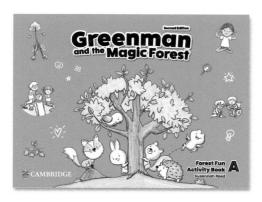

Learning with *Greenman and the Magic Forest*

New Forest Fun Activity Book

This unique **Activity Book**:

- is strongly influenced by a forest school approach and promotes child-centred, hands-on learning, related to the world around us.
- connects thematically to the Pupil's Book, but has its own structure, making the material flexible and suitable for use either in the classroom or at home.
- is easy to use and can help create the home-school connection that is vital for pre-primary aged children, as parents and carers can enjoy doing language practice, crafts and outdoor activities with their children, outside of class.

The Forest Fun Activity Books have been created in response to requests from teachers for additional pen-to-paper activities. Activities such as tracing, matching, colouring and drawing provide the fine motor skills practice essential for very young learners.

Activities that practise language and concepts from the Pupil's Book provide you with opportunities to evaluate comprehension, while craft activities offer learning through creative play.

The forest school concept enables teachers and parents to focus on well-being, with yoga-based activities and an emphasis on developing the whole child. The forest setting encourages children to connect with nature and the world around them, providing opportunities to go outside and appreciate their environment.

New Teacher's and Pupil's Digital Pack

The brand-new **Teacher's Digital Pack** is designed specifically for use in the pre-primary classroom:

- Presentation Plus software provides a digital version of each page of the main print components to display in class, and includes embedded audio and video.
- Interactive activities in each unit offer a change of focus and allow children to show you what they can do.
- Some pages of the Pupil's Book and Forest Fun Activity Book have an answer key, so children can compare the answers they have in their books with an example, encouraging them to start to become independent learners.
- Dynamic, attractive games provide a fun way to practise vocabulary, and Digital Flashcards and Routine Boards mean you have all the material you need for a successful pre-primary class at your fingertips.

The new **Pupil's Digital Pack** provides a home-school connection by enabling children to listen to songs and watch videos from the course at home.

Big Book stories

Reading in class should be a shared experience, and reading stories aloud from the **Big Book** mimics the way children engage with stories in their first language (L1). By interacting with stories, children develop essential oral language skills and learn to concentrate, follow a plot and ask questions.

- You can use the story time chant to transition into story time, so that children know what to expect each time you open the Big Book: *It's story time, story time, open the Big Book and look inside.*
- You could also create a comfortable story corner, with cushions, where pupils go to listen to a story.
- When you take out the Big Book, convey excitement with your facial expressions and comments – your enthusiasm for reading will be contagious.
- While reading the story, pause throughout and interact with the pupils. Point to pictures in the book to elicit vocabulary, e.g. *Oh, look! What's this?* Encourage pupils to count items, identify shapes, or repeat a word or phrase from the story when you point to it.
- Where necessary, you can use L1. If the children identify a picture or concept in L1, nod your head for positive reinforcement and say the word in English.

You can choose to read the stories from the Big Book yourself, or use the audio track. You can also show the animated story video to engage children and support understanding. In addition, each Lesson 3 has a pop-out activity, which reinforces comprehension of the story.

At the end of the unit, revisit the story to consolidate the language and values that have been learnt.

'Hello, Greenman,' says Tree.
'Hello, Tree. Have you got any plums?'
'Yes, I have.'
'Can I have some plums, please?'
'Yes. I like sharing my plums. Here you are.'
'Thank you!'
'One, two, three, four, five, six.'

46

Classroom routines

Starting the lesson

Start each lesson with some classroom routines. The new and improved Routine Boards on Presentation Plus are ideal for introducing routines to your class. Choose your routines from the ideas below or think of your own. You can build on these over time as pupils become more familiar with English lessons, but it's a good idea to repeat some each lesson to help pupils to feel comfortable. If they feel comfortable in their learning environment, they will be ready to learn!

- Ring a bell, tap a triangle or shake a tambourine to get the children's attention and signal the start of English class.
- Say *English time!* and clap for each syllable of the phrase. Repeat and encourage pupils to join in by clapping the rhythm.
- Call the pupils to the carpet for circle time. Say *Circle time, circle time, 1, 2, 3. Circle time, circle time, sit with me!* When the children are sitting, have Greenman hide behind your back and peek around you. Pretend that you can't see him. Teach the target language by saying *Where is Greenman? We want to say 'Hello'.* Use hand motions to show 'hello' and encourage pupils to join in. Wait for the pupils to say *Hello, Greenman* (encourage pupils with gestures). When the pupils say 'hello' to Greenman, he 'comes to life' with a big stretch and a sigh to greet the pupils. Encourage pupils to stretch with Greenman until he starts the class by saying *Good morning, class! Hello!* Model responses for the pupils to repeat *Good morning, Greenman! Hello!*
- Have Greenman sing the *Hello* song (see page 20) with the class. During the song, have Greenman 'look' at different pupils and encourage them to do the hand motions for the song. This should be a fun and engaging time!

- Show a box with realia connected to the theme of the lesson or unit. Open it up and invite different pupils to pull out items from the box and hold them up or pass them around. Encourage the rest of the class to guess what the lesson will be about.
- Place a piece of paper with a different colour on it on each table (e.g. yellow, blue, green, red). Hand out cards with one of the four colours to pupils. The pupils with yellow cards go and sit on the yellow table and so on. This helps ensure pupils work with different classmates throughout the year.

Routine songs

This is a time to review weather, seasons, birthdays, colours, numbers and shapes. You can use the Routine Boards or Flashcards on Presentation Plus, or draw pictures on the board.

First, Greenman announces the helper of the day (this could change daily or weekly, and you could choose pupils in alphabetical order or pull names out of a box). Say *(Mario), you are today's helper!* Encourage the class to clap and model teamwork skills by being happy for the chosen helper as he/she stands next to Greenman, e.g. *Very good, (Mario)! Congratulations!* Greenman's helper can help to select the correct elements on the Routine Boards, or point to the correct picture.

Say *What's the weather like today?* Sing the *Weather* song with the class.

Weather

Hey, hey, let's all say,
What's the weather like today?
Here we go! Here we go!
What's the weather like today?
Is it hot? Is it cold?
Is it sunny? Is it raining?
Is it cloudy? Is it windy?
Is it snowing?
Today it's ...
Today it's ...

Greenman or the class helper can point to the different weather elements on the board as the class say the types of weather. Encourage the class to join in saying *Is it snowing?* (pause and give clues by shaking your head) *No. Is it raining? No.* Continue until you find the correct type of weather. When the correct weather is found, the helper selects it on the weather Routine Board (or draws a circle around it on the board). Do the same to find the seasons.

You can also review colours and shapes with the Routine Boards and the audio. Ask pupils to point to the different colours when they are mentioned in the song and ask them to find the correct shapes on the shapes Routine Board.

 ## Colours

Look up, look down, and all around,
Colours, colours everywhere.
Look up, look down, and all around,
Colours, colours everywhere.

*OK, let's look for **black**!*
This is …
That is …

Look up, look down, and all around,
***Black** is everywhere!*
Look up, look down, and all around.
Colours, colours everywhere!

Repeat with: *white, brown, purple, pink, orange, grey*

 ## Shapes

Shapes, shapes, shapes, oh yeah!
Let's draw a shape in the air.
Are you ready?
*1, 2, 3! Draw a **circle** with me!*
Circle. Circle. Circle.
Let's go!

Repeat with: *triangle, square, rectangle*
Lots of lovely shapes!

If there are birthdays or special events, Greenman can lead the class in singing the *Happy birthday* song.

 ## Happy birthday

It's a very special day for somebody today!
Happy birthday to …!
It's a very special day for somebody today!
Happy birthday to …!
You're our friend and you are great!
So, we all want to celebrate!
Happy birthday! Happy birthday to …!

At the end of the class, Greenman says *Close your books, friends. It's time to tidy up!*

 ## Tidy up

Oh what fun, but now we're done!
It's time to tidy up!
All together, what a team!
It's time to tidy up!
Against the clock we have to race.
Put everything back in its place.
We don't want to leave a mess.
It's time to … tidy up!
x3 (faster each time!)
Last line: *It's time to, time to, time to, time to, time to … tidy up!*

Goodbye

Choose a lesson closing routine or routines to end the class.

- After the pupils have finished tidying up and have sat down in their places, be sure to have Greenman say *Goodbye* to individual pupils, saying each child's name if there is time.
- Sing the *Goodbye* song as a group, with or without the audio track (see page 21).
- Ring a bell, tap a triangle or shake a tambourine to signal that it is the end of English class and time to line up.
- Chant *Time to go! Time to go! Goodbye, goodbye, goodbye.* and clap for each syllable. Repeat and encourage pupils to join in by clapping the rhythm.
- Have pupils line up and encourage them to say a word in English as they leave. They can give you a 'high five' or a 'thumbs up' after they say their word. You can hold up a flashcard as a prompt and whisper the word, depending on the needs of your pupils.

How to structure your lessons

Greenman and the Magic Forest's lesson structure helps pupils to build their English comprehension. Its consistency and repetition allows them to predict what's coming next, building confidence and facilitating learning.

Starting the lesson

Have the **Greenman Puppet** greet the teacher and class. As Greenman only speaks English, the pupils associate his presence in the classroom with English time. Pupils will look forward to greeting the puppet, and this will prepare them to hear and speak English during the class. For other ideas for starting the lesson, see page 8.

Circle time routines

Introduce circle time using the Circle time chant: *Circle time, circle time, 1, 2, 3. Circle time, circle time, sit with me!* (motion a circular shape when you say 'circle time'). During this time, pupils will enjoy listening to, and joining in with, the routine songs to review the concepts of weather, shapes and colours on a regular basis (song lyrics can be found on pages 8 and 9). You can use the audio recordings for all the routines. While the pupils may not be able to say all of these things in a complete way, they will be passively learning the structures and sounds of the language through the songs.

Greenman Puppet

You can hold question and answer sessions using the **Greenman Puppet**, who invites pupils to join in and answer questions, including: *What's the weather like? It's (cloudy). Which season is it? It's (winter). Do we have any birthdays today? It's (Rebecca's) birthday! Let's sing Happy birthday to (Rebecca)!* Gradually, as the language becomes more familiar, pupils will feel comfortable enough to participate in the questions and answers, and by the end of the school year, they will be able to produce a great deal of the language.

Phonics review

Circle time is also a good time to review phonics sounds learnt in previous lessons, using the downloadable **Phonics Flashcards**.

Active time

Warmer

The next part of the lesson focuses on interacting with the different objectives of the lesson in a participative way. First, there is a 'warmer' which presents and reviews the unit vocabulary using the **Flashcards**.

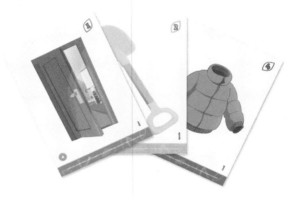

TPR

The warmer is followed by TPR activities that include songs, flashcards and games. Use the Stand up chant to transition between circle time and activities that require movement: *Stand up, stand up, 1, 2, 3. Stand up, stand up, tall with me!* (Stretch high on your tiptoes.)

The objective of active time is to have young learners identify English words or structures in as physical a way as possible. The more senses used and real life connections offered to pupils, the better. Many of these activities involve something with which pupils are already familiar, for example, working with the contrasting terms of *up* and *down* by playing a game in which the pupils jump up or crouch down low while the teacher says *up* or *down*. Adding English in this context is fun and meaningful.

Story time

Use the Story time chant to introduce story time: *It's story time, story time, open the Big Book and look inside.* (Motion opening a book.) By reading with pupils and sharing an enthusiasm for reading, you are encouraging pupils to enjoy reading themselves. While very young learners will most likely not understand every word used in the stories, they will be able to understand the main ideas and identify the characters and the basic storyline. *Greenman and the Magic Forest* provides stories that are appealing and relatable to pupils.

Lesson 1

Lesson 1 of each unit looks closely at one page of the **Big Book** story, usually the first page. Without going further into the story, the pupils can identify the theme of the new unit and begin to recognise the new vocabulary that Greenman has introduced.

Lesson 2

In Lesson 2, the complete story is read by the teacher, or listened to on an audio track, or both. There is also an animated **story video** on **Presentation Plus** that teachers can play so that pupils can watch as they listen to the story. The pupils answer questions (with help and prompting) related to the events in the story to practise the language of the lesson. The story is then reviewed in the other lessons of the unit.

✎ Table time

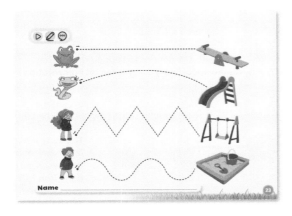

This is the time when children sit down at their tables to do some pen to paper activities. Use the Table time chant here to transition: *To the tables (to the tables), off we go (off we go). 1, 2, 3 quiet and slow!* The parentheses are an echo. Whisper the last phrase and count down.

Worksheet activity

The worksheet activities include colouring, drawing connecting lines, tracing different shapes, completing picture activities and matching stickers to vocabulary items. These activities help pupils make connections with the vocabulary, while making the worksheet activities feel like games. Pupils will build fine motor and pre-writing skills, as they draw, circle, colour and connect with lines. The clear illustrations make the activities simple and straightforward to explain to pupils.

Extra activity

There is an optional extra activity on the back of each worksheet to reinforce the lesson content and provide further opportunities for the pupils to be creative in the classroom. This is also a very useful tool for teachers to use with fast finishers.

Teacher Resources Worksheets

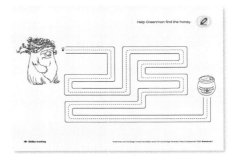

The **Teacher Resources Worksheets** include optional activities to further develop skills and connections during table time. There are four downloadable worksheets per unit which work on language, values, skills and phonics. Each review section contains two worksheets that show pupils how to make a seasonal project.

Forest Fun Activity Book

The **Forest Fun Activity Book** (AB) is aligned to the Pupil's Book without following the same structure. It provides further practice of some of the vocabulary, language and numbers taught, through activities that promote creativity and well-being. The AB teaching notes also provide opportunities for you to talk with pupils about nature and the environment around them.

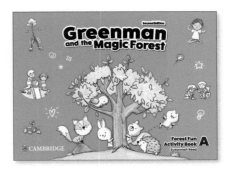

Home-school connection

Research shows the positive impact of involving parents and carers in children's learning. This can be achieved by:

- Sending home a downloadable **Letter to parents** at the start of each unit, to tell families what children will be learning.
- Creating an 'Our English Lessons' display in the drop-off/pick-up area, and keeping it updated to show the current unit topic, together with the children's work.
- Sending home completed **Pupil's Book** worksheets (the Pupil's Book has been specially designed so that pages can be torn out) or **Teacher Resources Worksheets** for families to view. You could also send home Teacher Resources Worksheets for pupils to complete at home, for extra practice.
- Encouraging pupils to share course songs, raps, stories and videos at home via **Home Practice: Videos and Songs** on Cambridge One. This is a great way of getting families to practise new language at home.

Unit walkthrough

Greenman and the Magic Forest has been developed to be used in pre-primary classrooms with 3–5 sessions a week, but is easily adapted to different amounts of teaching time. There are six main units per level, plus one introductory unit, four review units and four festival units.

Lesson 1: vocabulary

An **introduction video** on **Presentation Plus** introduces each unit topic, providing a fun way to engage children with the unit theme.

This worksheet is connected to the story and involves identifying, completing or drawing pictures of the key vocabulary to help pupils learn it.

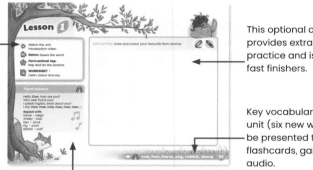

This optional activity provides extra vocabulary practice and is perfect for fast finishers.

Video, song, say and colour or draw icons help pupils understand what they will be doing in the lesson ahead.

Key vocabulary for each unit (six new words) can be presented through flashcards, games and audio.

Pupils practise the vocabulary through a song with TPR actions to support understanding, learning and retention. Reinforce learning by playing the **vocabulary song video** on **Presentation Plus**.

Lesson 2: structures

A downloadable **Teacher Resources Worksheet** provides extra practice of the key language.

This worksheet provides practice of the key vocabulary and language structures in the unit, as well as promoting fine motor and critical thinking skills.

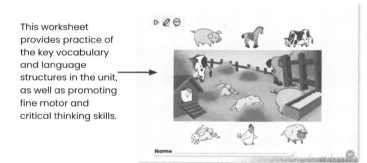

The story presents some of the key language from the lesson, so that pupils can listen to it being used in a 'real' context. You can read the story in the **Big Book**, play the audio version while pointing to the pictures, or play the **story video** on **Presentation Plus**.

Key language for each unit recycles the vocabulary from Lesson 1 and is based on language presented in the **Big Book** story. Games and role-play activities provide opportunities for practising the language.

Lesson 3: concepts

Pupils can listen to the story or watch the **story video** again to review the Lesson 2 language structures and explore the unit concept. There are also opportunities to talk about the emotions and value presented in the story.

This worksheet focuses on the unit concepts, as well as developing critical thinking skills.

Pupils can explore the unit concepts/ themes further by acting them out using the **Pop-outs**.

This optional activity provides extra practice of the unit concepts.

A downloadable **Teacher Resources Worksheet** focuses on the unit value and concepts.

Pupils will explore opposite concepts (such as *hungry/thirsty, good/naughty*) presented through the **Big Book** story. Understanding the opposites develops cognitive skills and gives pupils the tools to learn how to compare two different things.

Lesson 4: actions

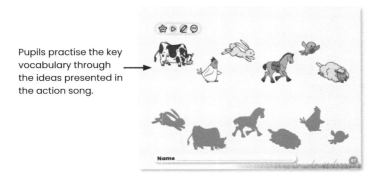

Pupils practise the key vocabulary through the ideas presented in the action song.

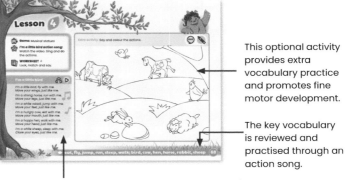

This optional activity provides extra vocabulary practice and promotes fine motor development.

The key vocabulary is reviewed and practised through an action song.

A TPR action song is presented through audio and an **action song video** on **Presentation Plus**. Children of this age group love movement and songs, so action songs are great for teaching and reviewing language, as well as developing gross motor skills and spatial awareness. Play the song many times for pupils to join in with the actions and some of the words. Each time you play the song, their confidence will grow and they will reproduce more words.

Lesson 5: skills

A downloadable **Teacher Resources Worksheet** provides pre-writing and/or number work reinforcement.

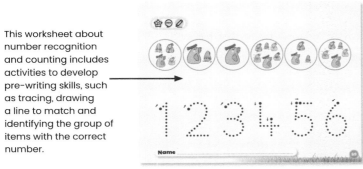

This worksheet about number recognition and counting includes activities to develop pre-writing skills, such as tracing, drawing a line to match and identifying the group of items with the correct number.

This optional activity provides additional number practice.

The numbers 1–6 are presented and practised through songs, counting games and on-page activities.

Each Lesson 5 has a fun song with a repetitive structure and actions to practise counting.

Lesson 6: consolidation

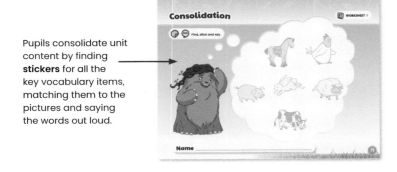

Pupils consolidate unit content by finding **stickers** for all the key vocabulary items, matching them to the pictures and saying the words out loud.

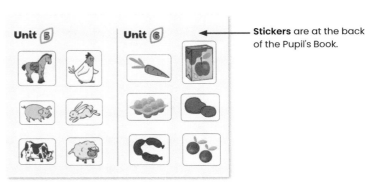

Stickers are at the back of the Pupil's Book.

Season review pages

Downloadable **Teacher Resources Worksheets** provide a seasonal craft project.

Pupils review the key vocabulary by identifying it and then categorising and matching it to a unit themed photo.

This optional activity practises key vocabulary and concepts alongside fine motor skills.

Season themed review pages (autumn, winter and spring) appear every two units and review vocabulary from the previous two units through flashcard activities and games. A summer review page appears at the end of the course and reviews vocabulary from all six units.

A seasonal song helps support pupils' understanding of the seasons and the world around them and introduces some seasonal words, such as *leaves* in autumn, as well as reviewing weather and colours vocabulary. The **Teacher's Book** provides actions to aid understanding.

Festival lessons

Four festival lessons allow pupils to explore special days and the ways in which they are celebrated. In Level A, festival lessons include World Peace Day, World Book Day, World Friendship Day and Green Day.

Pupils can hear the new vocabulary in a 'real' context through a dialogue or song, before colouring the vocabulary words to complete the picture. **Pop-outs** allow pupils to explore the festival further by acting out the dialogue/song. A downloadable **Teacher Resources Worksheet** provides a hands-on activity related to the festival.

Three new themed vocabulary words are introduced through audio and flashcards.

Forest Fun Activity Book

Pupils circle the unit forest animal on the Welcome page when they finish each unit.

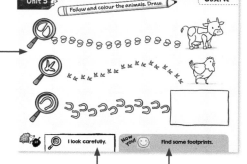

Activities are related to nature and the environment and promote creativity and well-being. Pupils are encouraged to practise skills and observe, find, feel, investigate and care for nature.

Yoga is great for improving concentration and memory, promoting mindfulness, helping children manage 'big' emotions and encouraging self-esteem. In three units, yoga poses are presented in one of the AB lessons. Optional **yoga videos** can be used as a model to help pupils try out these poses for themselves.

Pupils are encouraged to think about what they did well and to repeat an affirmation to build self-confidence and self-belief.

Optional 'Now you!' sections encourage pupils to interact with natural materials to make craft projects or explore nature outdoors.

Phonics in *Greenman and the Magic Forest*

Many pre-primary teachers recognise the usefulness of teaching phonics in their English classes. For this reason, *Greenman and the Magic Forest* provides a fully integrated phonics programme through the Extra Phonics Lessons.

What is phonics?

Phonics is a systematic method for teaching pupils the sounds and letters of English. The 44 phonemes in the English language are taught explicitly, rather than expecting pupils to hear them and 'pick them up'. By attaching a letter or letters to each phoneme, pupils learn to pronounce all of the sounds of the language at a very young age. Where once pupils used information from L1 to try to pronounce English words, they now recognise that the two languages are different and have separate pronunciation patterns.

How does it work?

Starting with the simplest letters (for example, the *s* in *snake*) pupils learn to recognise the most common sound associated with the letter. The letter and the phoneme combined are called a letter sound. Children begin by identifying words starting with the sound (*Stella, Sam, sun, star, school*). As there are 26 letters in the alphabet but 44 sounds, sometimes two letters are needed to show one sound. Some examples of these spellings are the *ai* letter sound in *rain* and the *oa* letter sound in *boat*.

Alternative spellings

The English language comes from many sources, so sometimes there is more than one way to spell a sound. An example of this is the *ai, ay* and *a_e* spelling patterns for the same sound (e.g. *rain, day, snake*). Of course, very young children find it difficult to read words with alternative spellings. In *Greenman and the Magic Forest* our objective is for pupils to say the sounds and recognise them in key vocabulary rather than read words.

Extra Phonics Lessons

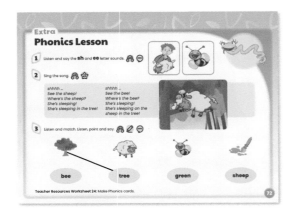

The course has a phonics lesson in every unit. Each lesson introduces one or two letter sounds through an audio recording and downloadable **Phonics Flashcards**. The Phonics Flashcards can also be accessed on **Presentation Plus** and used to help children remember and revise the letter sounds they have learnt. Since repetition and reinforcement is key to remembering the letter sounds, it's a good idea to include phonics practice between phonics lessons, as part of a daily routine.

Pupils also practise the letter sounds through engaging phonics songs. Point to elements in the pictures and use the actions suggested in the **Teacher's Book** to support understanding and recall of the target letter sounds.

Downloadable **Teacher Resources Worksheets** reinforce the phonics letter sounds through activities that develop fine motor skills.

The step-by-step lesson plans in the Teacher's Book are easy to follow and don't require phonics knowledge on the part of the teacher. Once you start using the phonics lessons, you will begin to get a feel for the method.

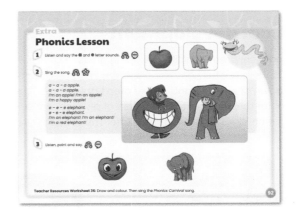

Each festival lesson also has an Extra Phonics Lesson. Letter sounds are presented through audio recordings and downloadable festival **Phonics Flashcards**. They are practised through a festival Phonics song and a listen and respond activity. Pupils listen to the letter sounds in an audio recording, identify matching words in the pictures and repeat the sounds and words. A downloadable **Teacher Resources Worksheet** for each lesson provides additional practice.

Supporting the pre-primary learner

Teaching very young children can be one of the most rewarding teaching experiences, but also one of the most challenging. For many children, pre-primary will be not only their first education experience, but also the first time they are away from their parents. It is also a change to their normal routine, all of which makes it an emotional time.

We are most able to support our learners when we know them and know what to expect from them. Children of this age:

- love to use all their senses to explore the world around them;
- need lots of praise and encouragement as they explore and learn;
- are learning to recognise how others are feeling;
- are imaginative and sensitive to people's behaviour towards them;
- feel safe in repetitive, nurturing environments, where routines are predictable and there are opportunities for skills to be practised;
- have short attention spans and need frequent changes of activity to stay focused;
- can't sit still or work on their own for long periods of time and need lots of guidance from the teacher.

For this age group, it is especially important to be patient and flexible, and to use lots of praise and positive reinforcement. Consider how you can:

- be clear about your expectations and the role of the children;
- create a visual, print-rich environment;
- build class routines;
- support learning through play.

Between the ages of three and six, children develop many different skills and it is important to recognise their stage of physical, cognitive, emotional and social development.

Physical development

Pre-primary children are still developing gross-motor skills and their balance is not fully developed. Some children are able to hop up and down on one leg and others aren't able to yet. To support gross-motor development, include lots of physical activities with actions for children to follow and imitate. The songs in *Greenman* *and the Magic Forest* are perfect for this and suggested actions are provided in the Teacher's Book.

Fine-motor skills also need practising. Many children still have difficulty in holding a pencil or crayon correctly, so tracing lines, shapes and zigzags in worksheet activities help children to gain this control. *Greenman and the Magic Forest* provides lots of pre-writing practice, as well as suggested craft projects which involve painting, cutting and sticking.

Cognitive development

Most pre-primary children cannot read or write. Learning at this age depends on repetition, physical response, movement and song, so *Greenman and the Magic Forest* focuses on teaching language through songs and stories, with audio recordings and videos to model language.

For most children, this is their first contact with a foreign language. They need time to experience the language receptively first, by listening to the sounds, the rhythm and the intonation. This is often called 'the silent period' and it is a crucial part of language learning because it enables children to internalise the language first. When the children are ready, they begin to reply with one-word responses which will gradually build up to small chunks of language.

Emotional and social development

Very young learners may initially be upset when they start school because it's a major change to their usual routine. We can help children to adapt and develop by being a caring role model and creating a nurturing environment that provides for their developmental needs.

At this age children:

- copy adults and classmates;
- are often egocentric and need activities that promote sharing and team work;
- begin to understand the concept of *mine*, *his* and *hers*;
- begin to take turns in games;
- show concern for a crying friend;
- can't always recognise the difference between real and make-believe;
- show a wide range of emotions;
- like to sing, dance and act out what they see around them.

Understanding where children are on their developmental journey will help you provide a safe learning environment for them to practise skills and explore areas of knowledge.

Promoting learning through play

Play is essential in children's development; they make sense of the world around them by imitating and acting out everyday actions and routines. It's through play that they connect with their classmates on a social level. They also learn key life skills, such as collaboration, cooperation and turn-taking.

Teacher-guided play, such as circle and TPR activities, works well in pre-primary classrooms. Clear instructions are given and boundaries are set. However, it can be beneficial to also provide opportunities for child-guided play to take place, where relevant toys, games and other materials are provided by the teacher, but children are left to choose which they play with and how they play with them. This can be a chance for you to observe:

- the way pupils interact with each other;
- the language being used (and to provide words or phrases in English, where appropriate);
- pupils' interests (which can inform the type of activities and learning environment you provide in the future).

To promote successful learning through play:

- use as much English as possible in teacher-guided games, until this language becomes a routine part of play;
- encourage pupils to make choices about play, e.g. allow them to bring toys to class that are relevant to the language you are teaching;
- monitor play and suggest ideas or words, without leading directly;
- allow pupils to control play, for example take turns as 'leader' and adapt the game;
- encourage pupils to play in groups or pairs once they are familiar with a whole-class game;
- create a dedicated English play area in the classroom, surrounded by English storybooks and toys related to the unit language/themes;
- make a home for Greenman in your English play area, so that pupils can interact with him freely.

Using L1 and English

The pre-primary classroom can be an ideal place to create an English-speaking environment. From the first moment, we can begin to use high-frequency 'chunks' of language, such as *stand up, sit down, find your book, How are you?*, which become familiar to pupils through constant repetition. You can also tell pupils that Greenman doesn't speak their L1, so they will expect him to always speak English to them.

However, we need to use plenty of visual prompts, such as flashcards, realia, mime and gestures, to ensure that children don't feel lost or overwhelmed. It may also be useful to use L1 on some occasions, for instance, if a child is upset or unhappy because of an argument with a classmate. L1 can also be used if you have first explained or demonstrated an activity using English, but feel that the children haven't understood. Sometimes L1 will be necessary if you wish to talk about a topic in greater detail, e.g. one of the values or emotions from the stories or ideas about caring for the environment. Such discussions are important for developing children's self-confidence, critical thinking skills and knowledge and understanding of the world. Repeat the children's ideas back to them in L1, to check you have understood, and then translate key words and phrases into simple English.

Games bank

Greenman and the Magic Forest offers games that can be adapted for different topics, vocabulary sets and language structures. Using games and movement in the classroom engages pupils and improves learning and retention.

Air drawings

This game can be used to practise shapes and adjectives. Draw a big triangle on the board. Say *What is it?* Elicit the response *Big triangle.* Say *Draw a big triangle in the air.* Model how to do this and repeat with other shapes until the pupils no longer need the example on the board. Monitor to help pupils who may be struggling.

Next, have the pupils draw the shapes in the air as you say them. Model how to draw them with your finger in the air. Say *Let's draw a small circle.* Show them how, and encourage those who have done it to help the other pupils to do the same. Repeat with other shapes and vary the sizes.

Draw the word

Have pupils sit in a circle, each facing the back of another child. Dictate a word or number and the pupils practise drawing it on their friend's back.

Find the number

Have pupils sit in a big circle on the floor. Prepare different classroom objects (pencils, crayons, books, etc.) making sure you have four to six of each. Place the objects in the centre of the circle. Choose small groups of pupils to find the correct number of items. Say *(Mario), (Lucía), (Iván), can you give me three crayons?* Have the pupils repeat *Here you are* after you as they hand you the objects. Repeat with different objects and different groups of pupils. To play the game in smaller groups, rather than as a class, prepare homemade number cards before the lesson. Give out one set of number cards for each group of four to six pupils, and have pupils take turns to choose a number card. When you say an item, the pupil whose turn it is counts out the same number of that item as they have on the number card.

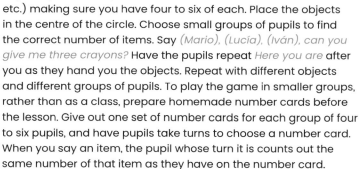

Hide and seek

This game can be played using the flashcards or other realia, and practises the unit vocabulary and basic prepositions. Place the flashcards around the classroom. Have the pupils close their eyes while you hide Greenman somewhere by a flashcard. Say *I will hide Greenman,* (hide him behind your back to show 'hide') *You will close your eyes* (cover your eyes) *open them* (uncover your eyes) *and say ('slide') if Greenman is here* (walk Greenman to the slide flashcard). Say *OK, close your eyes.* (put Greenman by a flashcard) *Open your eyes. Where is Greenman? The sandpit? No. The seesaw? No.* Continue until children have 'found' Greenman. Repeat with other words.

Jump to the word

Use the unit flashcards or draw pictures of the target vocabulary items on the board. In this game, pupils jump to the correct word and touch it. Choose one volunteer to demonstrate. Model the game yourself, first. Say *Let's play a game. I say a word: (slide)! You jump to the board and touch the picture. (Mario), let's play. Touch (slide).* Help the pupil by continuing to model what to do. When he/she has touched the correct picture, say *Well done! Let's line up to play!* Have the pupils line up and take turns jumping and touching the word that you say. If a pupil chooses the incorrect picture, help him/her to find the correct one.

Pass, stop and say

This game can be used to revise the vocabulary for one or several units. Have pupils stand or sit in a circle. Give out one flashcard to each pupil (or as many flashcards as you want to practise). Say *Now, pass the flashcards. Go.* Have pupils pass the flashcards around the circle (all in the same direction) until you say *Stop!* Say the name of one (or several) pupil(s) and have them say the word for their flashcard(s). Then tell the pupils to pass the flashcards again. Continue until all pupils have had a turn at saying one word.

Pass the ball

Have pupils sit in a circle. Take out a soft ball from a hiding place. Place the unit flashcards in the centre of the circle, face down. Say *Let's play a game. Let's pass the ball.* Pass the ball to your right and motion for the pupils to continue passing the ball. When the ball returns to you, say *Stop!* Pick up a flashcard from the centre, turn it over and say the word. Say *Now you!* Repeat the same process but this time stop on a pupil. Help the pupil to choose a flashcard and say the word. Practise one more time in the same way. Next, turn on lively music as the pupils pass the ball, and stop the music when you say *Stop.* Repeat until all the pupils have had a turn.

Point to the word

Stick the unit flashcards on the walls around the classroom. Sing the unit song and have pupils point to the different items when they hear the word in the song. Say *Point to the picture!* Model how to do this the first time you play the song, then have pupils join in.

Remember the cards

In this game pupils practise unit vocabulary with the flashcards. Hold two cards out for about five seconds, and then turn the cards around. Say *What is this?* indicating one of the cards. Call on a volunteer to come up to point to the back of one of the cards and say the word. If he/she guesses correctly, turn the card around. Call on another volunteer to guess the other card.

Add a third card or shorten the time if the class guesses the words very easily.

Roll and review

Place the unit flashcards in a horizontal line on the floor, leaving a space below them (about one metre). In this game pupils roll a soft ball to one of the cards and say the word. If the ball doesn't land on a card, they say the word closest to the ball. Say *We're going to play a game. I stand here* (point to the place on the floor where pupils should stand) *and roll the ball.* (roll the ball gently) *I say this word* (point to the card closest to the ball). Repeat with different pupils rolling the ball and saying the words until most have had a turn.

Roll and say

Have pupils sit in a big circle on the floor and set out the unit flashcards in a smaller circle in the middle. In this game pupils roll a big dice and move a counter around the circle of flashcards. When the counter lands on a flashcard, the pupil tries to say that word. Give pupils a counter each. Model the game first with one pupil, say *Roll the dice!* Have the child count the correct number on the face of the dice, and then move the counter the correct number of flashcards around the circle. The pupil then says the word/phrase for the flashcard that they land on. If the pupil struggles, act out the vocabulary or whisper the word. Repeat with different pupils until most (or all) have had a turn. Note: in the earlier units, pupils have not formally learnt the numbers 5 and 6, so you may wish to pre-teach them before playing. Alternatively, model saying the word when a pupil rolls one of these numbers and have pupils repeat after you. Have the class count out loud, as a pupil moves their counter around the circle.

Roll, jump and say

Set out the unit flashcards in a big circle on the floor. Roll a big dice and show the pupils the number. Say *A (five)!* Stand next to the first card and jump five cards around the circle, while counting. Then, say the word for the card you stop next to and have the pupils repeat the word. Say *(Lucía), it's your turn!* The pupil rolls the big dice and jumps around the circle the same number of cards as shown on the dice, and says that word. Repeat until most (or all) pupils have had a turn.

Run to the word

This game practises the unit vocabulary, using the flashcards. Have pupils sit in a large circle and place the flashcards face up in the centre of the circle. Choose a volunteer to model the game with you. Have Greenman say a vocabulary word (for example, *peg*), and run with the volunteer to touch the word. Exaggerate your movements to clearly show the volunteer what to do. Say *Well done! Class, repeat (peg).* Now, call on two pupils to 'run' to the next word. Repeat with each flashcard and different groups of pupils. Encourage pupils to say *Well done!* after their classmates' turns.

Show me!

This game practises the vocabulary for emotions. Put both hands in front of your face and say *One, two, three. Let's make a (happy) face!* Uncover your face and show your 'happy' expression. Gesture to show that you are going to do the expressions all together as a class (for example by motioning in a circle to include everyone). Now, the pupils cover their faces at the same time as you. Repeat the same emotion first and follow with other emotions pupils know.

Show the number

This game practises numbers and classroom objects. Say a sentence such as *There are three pencils.* and have pupils hold up the correct number of items. Prepare pupils for the activity by passing out enough pencils (or another item) for each child to hold up four (or more). Say *There are three pencils.* Help one pupil to count and hold up three pencils. Encourage the other pupils to do the same. Repeat with different numbers.

The hoop game

This game is similar to the fairground game in which you throw a hoop onto a bottle. In this case, pupils throw a hoop onto a flashcard on the floor and say the word.

Place the flashcards face up on the floor. Model how to throw a hoop, in a horizontal position, to land on a flashcard. Say the word, then say *OK, (Mario), now you!* Have the pupil repeat the activity as you have modelled. Continue until all or most pupils have had a turn.

Touch the colour

This game can be played with any group of colours. If working with pink and purple, for example, set out pink and purple objects. Say *This is pink, repeat, pink. This is purple, repeat, purple.* Repeat this two more times. Choose a volunteer and say *Touch purple.* Show 'touch' by gesturing with your index finger. Help the pupil if he/she struggles. Choose another volunteer to touch a colour. Repeat with several pupils.

Welcome Unit: Let's be friends!

Lesson 1

Lesson objective
To review basic greetings, introductions and vocabulary from *Greenman and the Magic Forest* Starter Level.

Language
New: *Greenman, Nico, Sam; Hello, I'm (Sam).*
What's your name?
Review: colours; numbers 1–3
Receptive: *Let's (point). What colour is (Greenman)?*

Materials
Presentation Plus, Greenman Puppet, PB page 5, Class Audio, crayons, pencils. Optional: PB page 6, ball

🖊 Starting the lesson

To start the lesson call the pupils to the carpet for circle time. Say *Circle time, circle time, 1-2-3. Circle time, circle time, sit with me!* When the pupils are sitting, have Greenman hide behind your back and peek around. Pretend that you can't see him. Teach the target language by saying *Where is Greenman? We want to say 'Hello.'* Use hand motions (e.g. waving) to show 'hello' and encourage pupils to join in. Wait for the pupils to say *Hello, Greenman* (encourage them with gestures). When the pupils say 'hello' to Greenman, he 'comes to life' with a big stretch and a sigh to greet the pupils. Encourage pupils to stretch with Greenman until he starts the class by saying *Good morning, everyone! Hello!*

Next, Greenman will start the *Hello* song with the class. During the song have Greenman 'look' at different pupils and encourage them to participate by waving or clapping. This should be a fun and engaging time!

 🎵 **Hello song**

Put your hand up if you're ready,
Wave and say hello!
Hands together if you're ready,
Come on then ... let's go!
The magic forest waits for you
Greenman, Sam and Nico, too!
Hands up, hello, clap, clap, let's go!

🖊 Routines

Settle the class with an opening routine (see Teacher's Book pages 8 and 9).

🖊 Active time

Warmer

Use the Greenman Puppet to model a dialogue to say 'Hello' and introduce yourself. *(Hello, How are you? What's your name?)* After demonstrating this dialogue yourself, call up volunteers to have the conversation with Greenman.

Say the names.

Sitting in a circle, pupils will introduce themselves to the child next to them, in turn. Model first with Greenman. Say *Hello, I'm (teacher). What's your name?* Have Greenman respond *Hello, (teacher), I'm Greenman.* Then have Greenman turn to the next child beside him in the circle and say *Hello, I'm Greenman. What's your name?* Say to the child *Now you.* Say the words quietly to help the pupil *Hello, Greenman, I'm (Mario).* (Mario) then turns to the child on his right and introduces himself and asks *What's your name?* Continue around the circle with each pupil in turn saying 'hello' and introducing themselves to the person beside them.

Greenman and the magic forest song: Listen and sing.

Say the Stand up transition chant *Stand up, stand up, 1-2-3. Stand up, stand up tall with me!* Say *English is fun! I like English. We can go to the magic forest with Greenman! Let's sing a song.*

Play the song once through, modelling the actions. Then sing the song line by line and have pupils repeat the words and actions. Go through this more than once. Next, play the audio track and continue modelling the actions for pupils to follow. Repeat the audio track many times for pupils to join in.

 Greenman and the magic forest

Welcome to the magic forest.
(Stretch your arms out wide and tall.)

Hello, hello, hello! (Wave 'hello'.)

Greenman and the magic forest.
(Move your hand from one side to the other as if displaying something very big.)

Come on! Let's go! ('Come' hand gesture.)

Let's go to the magic forest.
(Motion for someone to follow.)

Hello, hello, hello! (Wave 'hello'.)

Greenman and the magic forest.
(Move your hand from one side to the other as if displaying something very big.)

Come on! Let's go! ('Come' hand gesture.)

Greenman and the magic forest.
(Move your hand from one side to the other as if displaying something very big.)

Come on! Let's go! ('Come' hand gesture.)

🍃 Table time

Say the Table time chant *To the tables (to the tables), off we go (off we go). 1-2-3 quiet and slow!*

📖 Pupil's Book page 5. Worksheet 1: Colour Greenman, Nico and Sam.

Show pupils page 5 in the Pupil's Book and walk around to check that everyone is on the correct page. Hold your own book up for pupils to see. Pupils will identify the characters in the book, say their names and colour them. Say *Where's (Greenman)? Let's point to (Greenman).* Elicit or introduce the other characters (Nico is the boy and Sam is the girl) and have pupils count them. Say *What colour is Greenman?* Elicit the colour *Green.* Say *Let's colour (Greenman).* Model how to colour Greenman in your own book, then give pupils time to colour the other characters. Monitor pupils as they work.

🍃 Goodbye

To end the lesson, Greenman says *Close your books, friends. It's time to tidy up!* Model tidying up and gesture for the pupils to participate. You may wish to sing the *Tidy up* song (Track 6, Teacher's Book page 9) first or, alternatively, play it while pupils are tidyng.

After the pupils have finished tidying up and have sat down in their places, be sure to have Greenman say 'goodbye' to different pupils, saying each child's name, if there is time.

Next, sing the *Goodbye* song as a group, with or without the audio track.

 Goodbye song

Thank you, Nico. Thank you, Sam.
Thank you, Magic Forest and Greenman.
See you soon in English class.
It's time to say goodbye.

Bye bye, goodbye.
Bye bye, goodbye.
Bye bye.
It's time to say goodbye!

🍃 Extra activities

📖 Pupil's Book page 6. Extra activity: Trace and colour Greenman.

Hold up the Pupil's Book page for everyone to see, and walk around to check that all pupils have found the correct page. Hold up the Greenman Puppet. Say *Here's Greenman. Let's finish Greenman in the book. Trace the lines.* Model how to trace the lines in your own book and colour. Monitor the pupils and offer help as they work.

Game: *What's your name?*

Sitting in an open circle, say *What's your name?* and roll a ball to a pupil across from you. When the pupil has responded, say *Now you say, 'What's your name?'* Help the pupil or say the question along with them and mime for them to roll the ball to another classmate. Repeat this process until all of the pupils have participated. Practise going quickly or slowly between responses to make the activity more challenging.

Lesson 2

Lesson objective
To review basic greetings, introductions and vocabulary from *Greenman and the Magic Forest* Starter Level.

Language
Review: colours; family (*brother, daddy, mummy sister*); numbers *1–4*; toys (*doll, teddy, train*)
Receptive: *What is it? Point. Let's (count).*

Materials
Presentation Plus, PB page 7, Class Audio, 4 pictures each of: teddies, dolls, trains, brothers, sisters, mummies, daddies, crayons, pencils.
Optional: PB page 8, AB pages 2 & 3

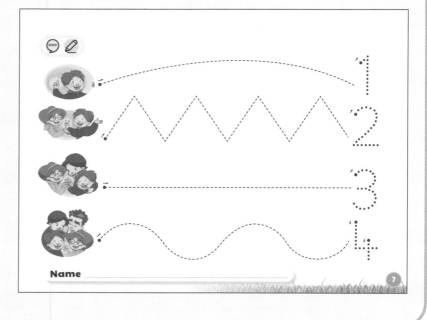

Name _____

🐾 Starting the lesson

Settle the class with an opening routine (see Teacher's Book pages 8 and 9).

🐾 Active time

Warmer

Review toy and family vocabulary from Starter Level. Draw pictures of the featured vocabulary on the board ahead of time (*teddy, doll, train, brother, sister, mummy, daddy*), or use the flashcards for these words from the Starter Level, if you have them. Point to the first picture. Say *What is it?* Elicit the response *A teddy.* Repeat with the other pictures. Practise identifying the words by saying *Point to the (teddy)* for pupils to point to the correct picture.

Look and count.

Take out the groups of vocabulary pictures that you have prepared. Lay out three pictures of trains and say *What is it? A train! Let's count! One, two, three. Three trains!* Repeat with the other vocabulary words varying the numbers each time. If the pupils are able, call up volunteers to count and name the vocabulary.

Game: *Jump to the word*

Use the pictures you've drawn on the board (or stick the flashcards to the board). Follow the description on page 18.

🐾 Table time

Say the Table time chant (see page 11).

📖 Pupil's Book page 7. Worksheet 2: Count and trace.

Show pupils page 7 in the Pupil's Book and walk around to check that everyone is on the correct page. Alternatively, ask pupils to hold up their books to show you that they have the correct page. Hold your own book up for pupils to see. Say *Where's Nico? Let's point to Nico.* Point to Nico on the first line. Say *Let's count. One! Let's trace the line to the number 1.* Model how to trace the line that leads to the number *1*. Repeat this for the different people and numbers in each line. Monitor pupils as they work. You may also want to model how to trace the numbers and take this opportunity to review the numbers *1–4*.

🐾 Goodbye

To end the lesson, play the *Tidy up* song (Track 6) and the *Goodbye* song (Track 8). Choose a closing routine and follow the description on page 9.

📑 Pupil's Book page 8. Extra activity: Count and colour.

Show pupils page 8 in the Pupil's Book and walk around to make sure that everyone is on the correct page. Say *Point to a doll. How many dolls are there? One, two! Well done.* Model how to count the dolls in your book. Say *What colour can we make the dolls?* Elicit responses from several pupils. Respond to each by saying *Good (Mario), you can make your dolls (blue).* Repeat the process with the other items in the picture. Then say *Let's colour.* Monitor the pupils and offer help as they work.

Game: *Count and clap*

Practise saying numbers and having the pupils count that number of times. Say *Let's clap one time, one* (clap once) *two* (clap twice). Continue to *four*. To begin with, clap along with the pupils. Once they are more confident in the activity they can clap on their own. Continue the activity saying the numbers in random order. You may also choose to have a volunteer take over your role and say the numbers.

Game: *Point to the number*

Put the groups of pictures you have made for the lesson around the room in groups of different numbers from one to four. Tell pupils to look for a number and item in the classroom, say *Find three trains!* Pupils point to the correct items. You could get progressively faster to increase the challenge.

✏️ Activity Book pages 2 & 3

Use the spread to introduce the idea of forest school – where pupils learn together and play outside. Talk about the picture in English and Language 1 (L1), asking pupils what they can see, and what the children in the forest school are doing.

Tell pupils (in L1) that when they use the Forest Fun Activity Book, they are going go to forest school as well. Use the pictures in the box at the bottom of each page to introduce the names of the forest animals in English (*rabbit*, *frog*, *squirrel*, *bird*, *hedgehog*, *fox*). Tell pupils (in L1) that the same forest animals are hiding in the main picture. Pupils find and colour them in. Then give pupils time to draw a picture of themselves in the scene.

Return to this spread at the end of each unit and have pupils circle the unit animal in the box. For example, when they finish Unit 1, they circle the rabbit. By the end of the book, pupils should have circled all of the animals.

Unit 1: Four rabbits

Lesson 1

Lesson objective

To introduce the main vocabulary for the unit (the classroom).

Language

New: *bag, board, computer, door, peg, window*
Review: *colours*
Receptive: *Where is the (board)? A rabbit. Colour (the picture).*

Materials

Presentation Plus, Greenman Puppet, Big Book story Unit 1, PB page 9, Flashcards Unit 1, Class Audio, sticky tape/tack, rabbit stuffed toy/picture, crayons, pencils.
Optional: PB page 10, AB page 4

 Use Presentation Plus to watch the unit introduction video and vocabulary song video. ▷

🖦 Starting the lesson

Settle the class with an opening routine (see Teacher's Book pages 8 and 9).

🖦 Active time

Welcome to Unit 1

▷ Tell pupils that you are about to start a new unit. Play the Unit 1 introduction video to introduce the unit topic. Pause the video at different points and ask, in L1, what the children can see and what they think they will learn about in this unit.

Warmer

Present Unit 1 Flashcards by holding them up and having the Greenman Puppet say the words with the pupils.

Find the classroom items.

Have sticky tape prepared to put on the back of each flashcard. Have Greenman hold up a flashcard and say the word. Model how to repeat after Greenman. Go through the group of flashcards twice.

Now, repeat the word and go to the item in the classroom and stick the card to it, say *(Board), where is the (board)?* Look around the classroom, let the children point and feel in charge of helping you to find the item. Say *Oh, here it is, thank you! This is the (board).* Do the same with each item.

The Big Book story for this unit features the character Rabbit, who is hiding in the classroom. If possible, use a picture of a rabbit,

or a stuffed toy rabbit, and take it out from under your chair, or somewhere near you.

Say *What's this? A rabbit? A board, a computer, a door, a peg, a window, a rabbit?* Nod your head to show that the first items make sense, and use a confused tone and expression when you say 'rabbit'. Set the rabbit aside until Lesson 2, you will refer to it again when reading the Big Book story.

At this point, you may wish to use the audio of the unit vocabulary to listen and repeat as a class.

 bag, board, computer, door, peg, window

My classroom song: Sing and point.

Say *It's time for a new song! Let's stand up and sing.* Say the Stand up transition chant (see page 10). Play the track once. Gesture *1, 2, 3* with your fingers and say *Come and look, point with me.* Then point to each vocabulary object in the classroom when it's mentioned. Nod at children who join in. Then sing the song without the audio slowly to give all pupils time to point to each item. Play the song track at least two more times, encouraging pupils to join in and point.

My classroom

In my classroom I can see.
Point with me, point with me.
*I can see a **board**. Can you see?*
Point with me, point with me.
Repeat with: *computer, window, peg, door, bag*

▷ You may wish to watch the vocabulary song video at this point.

Story time

Say the Story time chant *It's story time, story time, open the Big Book and look inside* and motion opening a book. Open the Big Book to the first two pages of the Unit 1 story. Say *What do we see? Oh, look! (A board! A peg! A computer! A door! A window! A bag!)* Encourage pupils to repeat the words while remaining seated.

After identifying all of the vocabulary words, close the book.

Table time

Say the Table time chant (see page 11).

Pupil's Book page 9. Worksheet 1: Look, say and colour.

Have pupils open their books to page 9 to look at the same picture as you have opened in the Big Book. Say *Can you find this picture?* Walk around the class to help pupils find the correct page.

Hold up flashcards of the key vocabulary and have pupils point to the items in the picture and say the names. Alternatively, play, sing or watch the *My classroom* song (Track 11) again. Model how to point to each vocabulary word in the picture on Pupil's Book page 9.

Say *Oh no! The picture isn't finished! Colour the picture to finish it.* Gesture colouring in the board, door, peg, bag, computer and window frame to finish the picture. Hold up a pencil or crayon and wait for the children to hold up their pencils or crayons as well. Make sure everyone has yellow, red, light blue, dark blue, light green and dark green pencils or crayons. Monitor the pupils as they colour, talking about the different colours and offering support and encouragement.

Goodbye

Follow the description on page 9.

Extra activities

Pupil's Book page 10. Extra activity: Trace and colour the school.

Pupils use a pencil or crayon to trace over the lines of the school. Say *Trace the lines.* Model how to do this. Pupils can then colour the picture. Monitor the children as they work.

Game: *Run to the word*

Play this game with the unit flashcards. Follow the description on page 19.

Activity Book page 4 – Observe

Pupils look through the window in their classroom and say what they can see, using any English words they know and L1.

Use the picture in the book to introduce the idea of a forest window. Pupils trace the tree trunk and imagine what else the children in the picture are looking at through the forest window. Encourage them to share their ideas.

Pupils draw their favourite ideas into the forest window outline on the page and compare their drawings. They can also colour their pictures and compare the different colours they've used.

I use my imagination. Compare pupils' forest windows and praise them for using their imagination and thinking of so many different ideas. Pupils repeat the affirmation *I use my imagination* with you.

Now you! Pupils can go outside and observe nature. They sit in one spot and note what they can see, hear and smell around them, before drawing a picture. Alternatively, they could look out of a classroom window and draw what they can see.

Encourage pupils to think about how good it feels to observe nature, and how colours, sights, sounds and fresh air outside calm us down and relax us.

Lesson 2

Lesson objective
To present the key structures for the unit.

Language
New: *There are (three rabbits). There aren't (four rabbits).* classroom items
Review: colours; shapes; numbers 1–4
Receptive: *Where is (the board)? Where are (four rabbits)? Let's (count the rabbits).*

Materials
Presentation Plus, Greenman Puppet, Big Book story Unit 1, PB page 11, box with groups of 4 classroom objects (books, pencils, crayons), rabbit stuffed toy/picture, Class Audio, crayons, pencils. Optional: PB page 12, Teacher Resources Worksheet 1, AB page 5

 Use Presentation Plus to watch the story video. ▷

Name

🍃 Starting the lesson

Settle the class with an opening routine (see Teacher's Book pages 8 and 9).

🍃 Active time

Warmer

Say classroom vocabulary words and have pupils point to them in the class. Have Greenman say *Where is the (board)?* If pupils start to identify the words easily, you may speed up and change the order each time you go through the words. Place a rabbit (stuffed toy or picture) somewhere in the classroom and also ask them to point to the rabbit as a fun preparation for the Big Book story.

Game: *Draw the word*

Follow the description on page 18. Model the activity first and, when you play the game, go through each vocabulary word twice.

Game: *No, Greenman!*

Take out your prepared box with four books, four pencils and four crayons. Say *Greenman, there are (four) books.* Greenman puts (two) books on the floor. Make a confused facial expression to show the pupils that this is incorrect. Say *One, two. No, Greenman! There are four books, there aren't two books!* Have a volunteer

come up and take out two more books and count with the class: *One, two, three, four! That's right! There are four books! Well done!* Repeat this process with different items and different numbers. Have pupils repeat *One, two. There are (four books), there aren't (two books). One, (two, three, four). There are (four books)!* Use the same rhythm each time you say these lines to help pupils to repeat. Shake your finger and your head when you say *There aren't.* Nod your head and smile when you say *There are.*

🍃 Story time

Say the Story time chant *It's story time, story time, open the Big Book and look inside* and motion opening a book. Open the Big Book to the Unit 1 story, Four rabbits. Take a moment to review the vocabulary on the page by saying a word and asking a volunteer to come up to point to it.

In this story the children can join in and count the circles, triangles, squares, rectangles and rabbits. Use exaggerated gestures to express confusion when the teacher in the story hasn't noticed that a *real* rabbit is in the classroom.

Read the story or play the audio version (Track 12), pausing to use facial and hand gestures to help convey meaning.

▷ Alternatively, you may want to play the story video.

Four rabbits

Sam and Nico
are at school.
'Come in. Put your bag
on your peg,'
says the teacher.
'Let's count. One, two, three!'
'One, two, three!' count
the class.
'Well done! I'm happy!'
'Where's Rabbit?' says
Greenman.

'Let's count the circles!'
says the teacher.
'One, two, three!' count
the class.
'Let's count the squares!'
'One, two, three!'
'Let's count the triangles!'
'One, two, three'
'Let's count the rectangles!'
'One, two, three!'
'Well done! You are good!'

'Let's count the rabbits!' says
the teacher.

'One, two, three ... four!'
'Four...? There are
three rabbits.
There aren't four.'
'Oh, it's Rabbit!' says Sam.
'Oh no! It's Rabbit!'
says Greenman.

'There are one, two, three
rabbits,' says the teacher.
'There aren't four!'
'Rabbit, come here!'
says Greenman.

'Let's count the rabbits!' says
the teacher.
'One, two, three ... four.
On the chair!'
'Oh ...! There are four rabbits!
Naughty Rabbit!'

'This is Stella, Frog and
Hedgehog. And this is
Greenman!' says Nico.
'We are friends!' says Sam.
'Hello!' says the class.
'I'm sorry!' says Rabbit.

🍃 Table time

Say the Table time chant (see page 11).

📓 Pupil's Book page 11. Worksheet 2: Count and circle the four rabbits.

Show pupils page 11 and walk around to check that everyone is on the correct page. Say *Let's count the rabbits here.* Point to the first shelf. Count the rabbits on each shelf together, pointing at different groups in turn. Then say *Where are four rabbits?* Choose a volunteer to come up to the front and point in your book at the shelf with four rabbits. Say *Let's circle four rabbits.*

Model how to circle the correct picture. When they have all finished, have pupils hold up their books to show you the completed activity.

🍃 Goodbye

Follow the description on page 9.

🍃 Extra activities

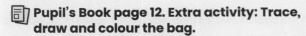

📓 Pupil's Book page 12. Extra activity: Trace, draw and colour the bag.

Pupils will trace the outline of the school bag and draw what they want to put inside using their imagination. Have them colour their bags.

Game: *Show the number*

Follow the description on page 19.

Teacher Resources Worksheet 1: Draw what comes next.

Pass out the worksheet, or ask your helper. Hold up your copy to show pupils how to point to each item. Say *Look, peg, bag, peg, bag, peg ... What comes next?* Help the pupils to say *bag.* Model how to draw the bag in the space provided. Repeat the process with *window/computer, door/board.* When they finish, pupils could point to the rows and say *There are (pegs). There aren't (doors).*

📖 Activity Book page 5 – Find and make

Pupils find natural materials and use them to make a picture for their classroom window. They can find the natural materials outside, either before or during the lesson, or you can bring the materials to class for pupils to find. In the autumn, it is a good idea to collect items like acorns and conkers to use later on in the year when they are harder to find. As well as the natural materials (twigs, leaves, bracken, flowers and grasses), you will also need string or twine (or paper plates), tracing paper, petroleum jelly or glue.

Point to the individual pictures in the book and describe the different natural materials in English and L1. Direct pupils' attention to the window collage in the book and tell pupils they are going to make one for their classroom window, using the natural materials.

Pupils look for the natural materials, either outside or among the materials that have been brought to the classroom. When they find one of the items in the pictures, they can circle it.

☺ **Now you!** Pupils then work in pairs to make the collage. Make the frames for pupils ahead of the class, by tying together twigs and gluing a sheet of tracing paper to the back. Alternatively, cut out and remove the middle of a paper plate and show pupils how to stick tracing paper between the two rims of the plate.

Pupils stick the leaves, flowers, bracken and grasses onto the tracing paper with glue or petroleum jelly. They can hang their pictures in front of the classroom window, so the sun shines through the natural materials.

🙆 **I am creative.** Tell pupils they are creative because they have used their ideas to make beautiful things. Pupils repeat the affirmation *I am creative* with you.

🌱 Help pupils understand the importance of the sun to plants. In this activity, it lights up the flowers in the window – but outside, the flowers, leaves and grass need the sunlight to grow.

Lesson ③

Lesson objective
To introduce a contrasting concept (good/naughty), and a value (being respectful).

Language
New: *good/naughty;* classroom items
Review: *happy/sad;* colours; shapes; numbers *1–4*
Receptive: *Look for differences. Rabbit is respectful. Circle (Nico).*

Materials
Presentation Plus, Greenman Puppet, Big Book story Unit 1, PB page 13, Pop-out Unit 1, paper 'smile', sticky tape, sleep mask/scarf, Class Audio, crayons, pencils. Optional: PB page 14, Teacher Resources Worksheet 2, AB page 6

 Use Presentation Plus to do the activity.

🔖 Starting the lesson

Settle the class with an opening routine (see Teacher's Book pages 8 and 9).

🔖 Active time

Warmer

Review emotions. Make a happy face and say *Happy.* Repeat with a sad expression. Next, say *Now, you. Be 'happy'.* Model a happy face for the pupils to imitate. Repeat with sad.

Game: *Show me!*

Play this game with *happy* and *sad.* Follow the description on page 19.

Game: *Place the mouth on Greenman*

Prepare in advance a paper 'smile' that pupils will be able to stick onto the Greenman Puppet with sticky tape. Take out the paper 'smile'. Invite pupils to guess what the activity will be. It may be familiar to them. Ask for a volunteer, and show how you will cover their eyes and they will put the paper smile on Greenman. Then cover the pupil's eyes and let them try! Say *Greenman is happy! He wants to smile!* Encourage each pupil and help the other pupils to do the same. You may want to say, e.g. *Oh no! A smile on Greenman's arm!* to express surprise when the pupils place the 'smile' in the wrong place.

🔖 Story time

Say the Story time chant *It's story time, story time, open the Big Book and look inside* and motion opening a book.

Take out the Big Book and read the story, stopping to point out parts of the story where we can see examples of 'naughty' and 'good' e.g. Rabbit on the bookshelf/the children sitting nicely. Point to the images and have the children make a thumbs up or thumbs down when you show 'good' behaviour or 'naughty' behaviour.

▷ You may also choose to use the video for the story, pausing the video rather than pointing to pictures.

🔖 Table time

Say the Table time chant (see page 11).

Do the pop-out activity.

Direct pupils' attention to the sample pop-out that you have prepared: Rabbit with a 'naughty' expression on his face under a chair, on one side, and Rabbit with a 'good' expression on his face sitting on the chair, on the other.

Say *Rabbit is good, he is respectful.* Show the pupils Rabbit being 'good' using your pop-out. Say *Look, he is naughty, now.* Show the pupils Rabbit being 'naughty'. Alternate showing the 'good' and 'naughty' sides of the Rabbit pop-out so the pupils can practise saying the words. Have them act out being 'good' rabbit and 'naughty' rabbit, while saying the words. Say *Now, you make Rabbit.*

Show pupils how to take out the pop-out carefully. Monitor as they do this and help as needed.

When all the pupils have finished, say *Show me naughty.* Hold up the pop-out, say *Show me good.* Model with your own pop-out. Continue alternating the words until all of the class is participating with the correct movements. Next, call on a pupil to take over your role. Give several pupils the chance to do this. You may also wish to reread the Big Book story or play the story video and have pupils hold up the correct side of their pop-outs at the relevant moments in the story.

Show pupils how to put away their pop-outs (in individual envelopes or in a common place in the classroom).

 Pupil's Book page 13. Worksheet 3: Find and circle the four differences. Then say _good_ or _naughty_.

Show pupils page 13 and walk around to check that everyone is on the correct page. Point to the two classroom pictures in your book, for the class to see. Say _Look for the differences. Look at the boy in this picture_ (point to the boy who is listening to the teacher). _Now, look at him in this picture_ (point to the boy looking behind him talking in class). _Here he is good, but here he is naughty._ (Point to the respective pictures.) Then say _Circle the boy._ Circle the boy in the second picture with your finger. Repeat with the other boy, Sam and Rabbit. In each picture, elicit _good_ or _naughty_ from the class.

🍃 Goodbye

Follow the description on page 9.

🍃 Extra activities

 Pupil's Book page 14. Extra activity: Draw your happy face.

Show pupils a prepared sample drawing for the activity. Say _This is my happy face. Draw your happy face._ Use gestures to convey meaning. Monitor pupils as they work.

Value activity: Being respectful

In the Big Book story some of the pupils are showing 'respect' for their teacher and classmates, and some are not. When reading the story and reviewing _good_ and _naughty,_ add the word 'respectful'. _Sam is respectful. She is good to her friends and her teacher. Rabbit is not respectful. He is naughty in the classroom._ At the end of the story Rabbit changes his attitude. Point this out and say _Hooray Rabbit! He's respectful!_ Point out the characters in the story being respectful and have the pupils come up to point.

Emotions: Feeling sorry

Look at the Big Book story again and ask _Is Rabbit naughty or good?_ Elicit that he is naughty. Then say _At the end of the story, what does Rabbit say?_ See if pupils can remember the phrase _I'm sorry,_ or say it for them to repeat. Explain, in L1, that feeling sorry means feeling bad about doing something naughty. Ask pupils when they feel sorry for doing something. You could give an example first, e.g. _I feel sorry when I don't listen to my friends. When do you feel sorry?_

Teacher Resources Worksheet 2: Trace and colour.

Pass out the worksheet, or ask your helper. Hold up your example, point to Rabbit and say _Rabbit is sorry. He says 'I'm sorry' to the teacher. Say 'I'm sorry' like Rabbit._ Model saying _I'm sorry_ for pupils to join in or repeat. Say _Let's trace Rabbit saying 'I'm sorry' and the teacher saying 'OK, Rabbit'._ Model an example by tracing the circle of dashed lines around Rabbit. When they have finished, pupils can colour in the pictures as well. Ask them about the colours they choose, as they work, or say _What does Rabbit say?_ to elicit the phrase _I'm sorry._

Activity Book page 6 – Practise

Bring (or ask pupils to bring) different shaped leaves to class. Uses the leaves to teach the word _leaf_ and revise numbers _1–4._

Model how to do the activity in the book by tracing number _1,_ counting the leaf prints and drawing a line to match the number _1_ to the correct number of leaf prints. Pupils continue the activity themselves.

🙆 **I am clever.** Check that pupils have traced and matched the numbers and leaf prints correctly. Praise them. Say _You can count to four. You are clever._ Pupils repeat the affirmation _I am clever_ with you.

🙂 **Now you!** Pupils do leaf printing in an indoor or outdoor classroom. Show pupils how to print with leaves by painting a leaf and pressing it down on paper. Pupils can choose different leaf shapes and colours to make their leaf prints.

🌱 Help pupils understand that different trees have different shaped leaves. Also tell them to use fallen leaves from the ground for this activity, and not to pick them from the tree.

Lesson 4

Lesson objective
To use TPR to review unit vocabulary through an action song.

Language
New: *Let's knock on the door. Let's open the window. Let's look at the computer. Let's wipe the board. Let's touch the peg.* classroom items
Review: *I'm happy!* colours
Receptive: *Roll the dice. Let's draw a line.*

Materials
Presentation Plus, PB page 15, Flashcards Unit 1, Class Audio, big dice (with the numbers 5 & 6 covered), counters, crayons, pencils, Optional: PB page 16, AB page 7

 Use Presentation Plus to watch the action song video. ▷

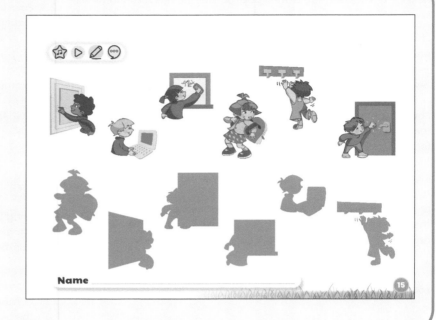

Name _____

15

🖦 Starting the lesson

Settle the class with an opening routine (see Teacher's Book pages 8 and 9).

🖦 Active time

Warmer

Show the Unit 1 Flashcards and have the children point to the items in the classroom all together. You can also have volunteers walk to the object to point to it.

Game: *Roll and say*

Follow the description on page 19.

Don't be sad action song: Watch the video. Sing and do the actions.

 You may prefer to use the action song video to teach the pupils the actions and the song.

First, play the audio and hold up flashcards for the vocabulary words in the song. Invite the pupils to say the word when you hold up the card. The second time you play the song, do the actions for the class. Next, have the pupils stand up *(Stand up, stand up, 1-2-3. Stand up, stand up tall with me)!* Teach them the actions one by one as you say each line of the song.

Practise the actions for the song three or four times slowly, going through the song line by line. Then play the audio track and do the actions together. Repeat until all of the class is participating in each action and singing some of the words.

🎧 13 Don't be sad

*Don't be sad, let's **knock on the door**,* (Shake your finger and make a sad face, knock on an imaginary door.)

Knock on the door, knock on the door. (Knock on an imaginary door.)

*Don't be sad, let's **knock on the door**,* (Shake your finger and make a sad face, knock on an imaginary door.)

Thank you! Now I'm happy! (Nod your head and make a happy face.)

Repeat with:

open the window (Motion opening a window.)

look at the computer (Touch next to your eye for 'look', type on an imaginary keyboard.)

put on your bag (Put on an imaginary backpack.)

wipe the board (Wipe an imaginary board with an imaginary eraser.)

touch the peg (Go on tiptoe and put one finger out to 'touch', do a motion as if hanging something on a peg.)

🍃 Table time

Say the Table time chant (see page 11).

 Pupil's Book page 15. Worksheet 4: Look, match and say.

Show pupils page 15 in the Pupil's Book and walk around to check that everyone is on the correct page. Sing or play the audio for the *Don't be sad* action song (Track 13). Model pointing to the actions shown on the worksheet as they are mentioned in the song. Say *What's this?* and point to the silhouette of the child putting on a bag. Say *Oh! Put on your bag* (do the action) *Let's draw a line to 'put on your bag'.* Show how to draw a line to connect the pictures. Have pupils say *put on your bag* and do the action. Repeat with the other pictures: *open the window, knock on the door, wipe the board, look at the computer, touch the peg.*

🍃 Goodbye

Follow the description on page 9.

🍃 Extra activities

 Pupil's Book page 16. Extra activity: Look, draw and colour three items.

In this worksheet pupils will choose and draw three of the vocabulary items, one inside each section of the school. Say the words and have pupils point to the pictures. Use gestures to show *draw* and *three*. Then have pupils colour their pictures. Fast finishers can add additional items if they wish. When they have finished, call out different vocabulary items and have the children stand up if they drew that item and sit down if they didn't.

Game: *The actions game*

Say an action from the *Don't be sad* action song (Track 13) and have children try to remember what the action is. Say *Show me (knock on the door).* Model the actions for the pupils to copy until the children begin to understand the game. Continue repeating different action words and do part of the action to help if pupils are having difficulty. Repeat with each action from the song until pupils are doing several actions without help.

📝 Activity Book page 7 – Care

Introduce the theme of tidying up. Emphasise the importance of keeping the environment around us (our home, our school, places outdoors) clean and tidy.

Direct pupils' attention to the school bags and have them count the bags in each picture. Say *It's a difference!* Pupils find and point to the other four differences and then circle all the differences. Note: You may wish to pre-teach number 5 before this lesson and then have pupils count all the differences at the end.

🧘 **I care for the environment.** Praise pupils for completing the activity and remind them that by keeping things clean we care for the environment around us. Pupils repeat the affirmation *I care for the environment* with you.

☺ **Now you!** Pupils can make a forest broom or duster (using a big stick, smaller twigs, and twine), and use it to clean their playground. Alternatively, they can help you pick up litter from the playground or tidy up the classroom at the end of class.

🌱 Help pupils understand why they shouldn't leave litter and why they should keep the outdoor environment clean for the animals that live there.

Lesson 5

Lesson objective
To work on pre-writing skills and practise numbers through a song.

Language
New: classroom items
Review: colours; shapes; numbers 1–4
Receptive: *Where's something (red)? How many frogs are there? Let's circle the (2).*

Materials
Presentation Plus, PB page 17, Flashcards Unit 1, Class Audio, homemade cards numbered *1–4,* 4 pictures of frogs or 4 frog toys, crayons, pencils, Optional: PB page 18, groups of 4 classroom objects (books, pencils, crayons), Teacher Resources Worksheet 3, AB page 8.

 Use Presentation Plus to do the activities and watch the Forest Fun Activity Book yoga video.

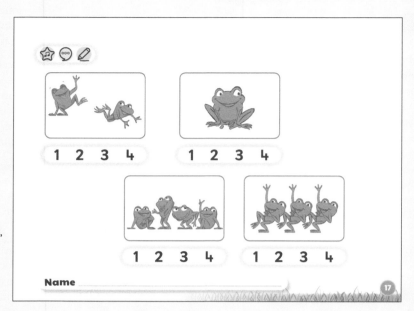

1 2 3 4   1 2 3 4

1 2 3 4   1 2 3 4

Name

17

🍃 Starting the lesson

Settle the class with an opening routine (see Teacher's Book pages 8 and 9).

🍃 Active time

Warmer

Review colours, shapes and numbers (you can use the Routine Boards or Flashcards on Presentation Plus to do this). After each topic, look for items around the room that represent it. For example, after reviewing all of the colours look for things in the classroom that are that colour. Say *Where's something red? The book is red!* Let the pupils look for other examples. For shapes, say *Where's something square? The windows are squares!* For numbers say *Where's something with two? I've got two eyes, one, two!*

Game: *Guess the number*

Prepare cards with the numbers *1–4* drawn on, before the class. Hold up each card *1–4* and say the number for the pupils to repeat. Choose a volunteer. Put a number card on his/her head so that he/she can't see it. Help the pupil to ask questions to guess the number. Model *Is it (two)? Is it (three)?* Help the other children to answer *yes* or *no* until the child guesses the number. Repeat with other volunteers.

Four little green frogs **number song 1–4: Sing and count.**

Say *Let's practise a new song with numbers.* Hold up the four frog pictures (or frog toys) that you have prepared. Say *We have four little green frogs, one, two, three, four! Let's sing the song.* Play the song.

 14 | **Four little green frogs**

> *4 little green frogs,*
> *Sitting on a log.*
> *4 little green frogs,*
> *1, 2, 3 and 4!*
> *1, 2, 3, 4!*
>
> *4 little green frogs,*
> *Sitting on a log.*
> *4 little green frogs,*
> *1, 2, 3 and 4!*

During the song, hold the frogs up one by one until you have four. After playing the song once, sing it without the audio and have the pupils repeat each line after you. Do this two more times, then play the audio track again. Repeat until the pupils are saying most of the words in the song.

Table time

Say the Table time chant (see page 11).

Pupil's Book page 17. Worksheet 5: Count and circle the correct number.

Show pupils page 17 in the Pupil's Book and walk around to check that everyone is on the correct page. Say *How many frogs are there? One, two! Let's circle the 2.* Model circling the number *2* with your finger. Continue with the other three pictures. Pupils can circle first with a finger, then with a pencil. As children finish, check their work.

Goodbye

Follow the description on page 9.

Extra activities

Pupil's Book page 18. Extra activity: Trace the numbers.

In this activity pupils will trace the outline of each number. Say *Find this page in your book.* Check that the pupils have found the right page. Say *Let's trace the number 1 with a pencil.* Model finishing the lines with your finger. Say *Now, let's do the number 2.* Continue until all the numbers have been completed.

Game: *Find the number*

Play this game with four of each item. Follow the description on page 18.

Teacher Resources Worksheet 3: Trace the pictures.

Pass out the worksheet, or ask your helper. Hold up a completed example to show the shapes within the objects. Say *What's this?* Say each shape and encourage pupils to repeat after you. Then, say *This side is the same as this side. Let's trace the lines.* Monitor pupils as they work, naming or eliciting the shapes as you circulate. You may choose to have pupils colour the shapes when they finish tracing. Ask any fast finishers to tell you the names of the objects (*door, ball, peg, computer*).

Activity Book page 8 – Feel

Look at the activity in the book. Teach the word *bee* and explain that the children are doing the bee yoga pose. Ask pupils to imagine a bee visiting flowers and have them make the noise of a buzzing bee.

Pupils then do the activity in the book – drawing their own face onto the second child doing the pose, and drawing the flower that the bee is visiting.

Now you! Have pupils stand up and do some stretching exercises with you. You can also do some simple yoga poses with them by reviewing poses pupils learnt in the Starter Level. Model how to do the bee pose and get pupils to copy you. Encourage them to imagine a bee visiting flowers while they do the pose. Pupils can watch the video for extra practice.

I feel calm. Relax your shoulders, smile and say *Oh – I feel good – I feel calm.* Ask pupils in L1 if they feel calm, too, and encourage them to say *yes.* Pupils repeat the affirmation *I feel calm* with you.

Help pupils learn about bees, and how they pollinate flowers. You may wish to plant bee-friendly plants, e.g. lavender or buddleia, in the school grounds.

Lesson

Lesson objective
To consolidate all unit content.

Language
Review: classroom items; Big Book language structures
Receptive: *march; Find and stick.*

Materials
Presentation Plus, Greenman Puppet, PB page 19, Flashcards Unit 1, Class Audio, Stickers Unit 1, crayons, pencils. Optional: AB page 9

🖥 **Use Presentation Plus to play the games.** ⊹☆

🔖 Starting the lesson

Settle the class with an opening routine (see Teacher's Book pages 8 and 9).

🔖 Active time

Warmer

Review the Unit 1 Flashcards by holding each one up and saying the word with the pupils. You may wish to use the audio of the unit vocabulary to review (Track 10).

March around the classroom.

March around the classroom with the pupils, stopping at each object from the unit. Pupils say the word. Say the Stand up chant (see page 10). Say *Line up for a game.* Use gestures and help the pupils to get into a line. Say *March, two, three, four, March two, three, four* until you arrive at a vocabulary item. Say *Stop! What's this?* Help the pupils to respond *Board!* Say *Very good, let's march! March, two, three, four. March two, three, four!* until you reach the next item. Continue until you have stopped at each item. Say the Circle time chant (see page 10) to call the pupils back to the circle.

🔖 Story review

Say the Story time chant (see page 10) and motion opening a book. Read the story again, inviting the pupils to participate in saying the words or lines that they know.

▷ Alternatively, you may want to play the story video.

🔖 Table time

Say the Table time chant (see page 11).

📑 **Pupil's Book page 19. Worksheet 6: Find, stick and say.**

Help the children to find page 19 of the Pupil's Book and locate the stickers for Unit 1. Say *Find and stick the pictures.*

Have Greenman repeat each word several times as the pupils look for the correct sticker to put in each place. Monitor the children

as they work and encourage them along, or give gesture clues. Repeat with each vocabulary word. When they have finished, have pupils point to each sticker and say the word.

🔖 Goodbye

Follow the description on page 9.

✏️ Activity Book page 9 – Investigate

Review the words *ant* and *egg* and remind pupils that ant eggs have baby ants in them. Ask pupils if they know where ants live.

Show a photo of an ant's hole or nest and ask pupils to think about what's inside it. Pupils then look at the book activity and find and point to the ants and the eggs in the nest. You may wish to explain the hierarchy of ant society (in L1): the Queen ant lays all the eggs and worker ants bring her food.

Have pupils finger trace the line from the hole at the top of the ant hill down to the egg chamber, then draw the line in pencil.

🙌 **I am interested in things.** Tell pupils that they now know what is inside an ant's home and that next time they see a line of ants, they will know where they are going. Remind pupils that it's good to be interested in things because it helps us learn about the world around us. Pupils repeat the affirmation *I am interested in things* with you.

🙂 **Now you!** Pupils can look for ant hills and observe the behaviour of ants after school with their parents as a home-school connection activity. Alternatively, take pupils outside and look for ants or other bugs. Allow time for pupils to observe the bugs and what they are doing.

🌱 Help pupils to understand that animals need a habitat and why we should protect them. Point out that a simple ant hole contains a very complex system of tunnels and chambers. We mustn't step on it or destroy it.

To end the unit, pupils circle the rabbit on page 2.

Extra Phonics Lesson

Lesson objective
To introduce two new phonics sounds ('a' and 'e').

Language
New: *ant, egg*

Materials
Presentation Plus, PB page 20, downloadable Phonics Flashcards, Class Audio, crayons, pencils. Optional: Teacher Resources Worksheet 4

🍃 Phonics time

Warmer

Review the phonics sounds from the Starter Level by pointing to the pictures on the Phonics Flashcards and having the pupils repeat the words. Either stretch out the target sound or have pupils repeat the sound in isolation.

Show the *a* (ant) and *e* (egg) Phonics Flashcards. Read the words, then segment the sounds. Say *Look at the picture: There is an ant. Listen to the sound: a. Listen and repeat: a–a–a–a—n-t.* Repeat with the second sound.

Point to the Phonics Flashcards and segment the sounds three times asking different pupils to repeat after you.

Pupil's Book page 20. 1. Listen and say the *a* and *e* letter sounds.

Have pupils open their books to page 20. Say *Point to the ant.* Say *a-a-a-ant* pointing to the picture. Repeat for the egg. Play the audio and have pupils listen and repeat the sounds and words. Repeat three times.

a – a – a	ant
e – e – e	egg

Pupil's Book page 20. 2. Sing the song.

Show pupils the picture in activity 2. Play the song. Point to items in the picture to help pupils understand the meaning. After playing the track three times, say it slowly, and have pupils repeat each line, while looking at the picture. Continue until pupils are saying at least the *Sam* and *The ants* parts of the song.

Sam has an apple,
Sam has an egg,
Sam has a bag,
On a red, red peg!

The ants have the apple,
The ants have the egg,
The ants have a picnic,
In the bag on the peg!

Pupil's Book page 20. 3. Listen, point and say.

Show pupils activity 3 in your book. Draw their attention to the written words *ant*, *bag*, *egg*, *peg* and *red*. Say the words in and out of order, and have pupils repeat after you. Then say, *Now listen, point and say.* Play the audio and model how to point to the pictures. Then play the audio again, pause when you hear each of the words and have pupils repeat, emphasising the target sound.

ant	bag	egg	peg	red
egg	ant	red	bag	peg
bag	peg	red	ant	egg

🍃 Extra activities

Teacher Resources Worksheet 4: Trace and colour the ants black and the eggs red.

Prepare one worksheet for each pupil in advance. Have the pupils practise saying the *a* and *e* sounds. Point to the pictures of the ants and eggs and say the words for pupils to repeat. On an example worksheet, model how to complete the tracing lines of the ants and the letter *a*. Say *Now you trace the ants and eggs. Trace the letters.* Monitor as pupils do this. Then say *Let's colour the ants black.* Have pupils hold up a black crayon before they start colouring. Repeat with the eggs and a red crayon.

Unit 2: The honey game

Lesson ①

Lesson objective
To introduce the main vocabulary for the unit (playground vocabulary).

Language
New: *sandpit, seesaw, slide, swing; bucket, spade*
Review: *colours; shapes*
Receptive: *Who is this? What colour is it? Take out your pencils.*

Materials
Presentation Plus, Greenman Puppet, Big Book story Unit 2, PB page 21, Flashcards Unit 2, Class Audio, crayons, pencils. Optional: PB page 22, AB page 10

 Use Presentation Plus to watch the unit introduction video and vocabulary song video. ▷

🌿 **Starting the lesson**

Welcome to Unit 2

▷ Tell pupils that you are about to start a new unit. Play the Unit 2 introduction video to introduce the unit topic. Pause the video at different points and ask in L1 what the children can see and what they think they will learn about in this unit.

🌿 **Active time**

Warmer

Have Greenman review colours and the names of the characters in the stories. Hold up the Big Book and point to Greenman on page 10. Ask *Who is this?* The children may say *Greenman* or perhaps point to the Greenman Puppet. Have Greenman say *Yes! It's me!* Have Greenman point to the other characters and repeat the question *Who is this?* and elicit the names for Sam, Nico, Stella and Frog.

Next review colours by asking about the colours shown on the page. Point to Greenman and ask *What colour is it?* Elicit the word *green.* You may also choose to have a volunteer come up and point to a colour when you say it. For example, say *What is green?* Help the pupil to find something green on the page to point to, like Greenman. Model how to point to the picture and say *green.*

Game: *Help Greenman!*

Have Greenman take out the Unit 2 Flashcards. Say *What are these Greenman? New words!* Act very excited about the new words. Take each flashcard out individually and say *Look! A (slide)! Repeat, class,*

a (slide)! What is it? A (slide). While you say the word, use gestures to reinforce the concept. Repeat this process with each card.

Have the pupils stand up. Say the Stand up transition chant *Stand up, stand up, 1-2-3. Stand up, stand up tall with me.* Show each flashcard again. This time have the pupils do the action that shows they are playing on/with that item. Say *How do we go on a slide?* Show a sample action. Look at the pupils' action and offer encouragement, such as *Oh, Lucía goes down* (do an action with your hand to show 'down') *a slide. Well done, Lucía.* Repeat the process with each card.

Now put Greenman where he can't 'see' the flashcards you hold up. Tell the pupils to act out each word for Greenman to guess. Say *Now, quietly* (hold your finger to your lips to show 'quiet') *show Greenman.* Hold up the card, model how to act it out and have Greenman shout the word. Congratulate the class for helping Greenman. Do the same with each flashcard.

At this point, you may wish to use the audio of the unit vocabulary to listen and repeat as a class.

 sandpit, seesaw, slide, swing; bucket, spade

The playground song: Sing and do the actions.

While pupils remain standing, play *The playground* song for the class. Hold up the corresponding flashcard when you hear each vocabulary word in the song. Encourage pupils to use their actions to show the word. Next, say the song line by line, slowly, enunciating the words and doing the actions. Then, play the song three more times, or until most pupils are participating by doing the actions and singing some of the words.

The playground

Come to the playground, (Gesture with your arm for people to follow.)

Play with me! (Run on the spot.)

Up and down, (Stand up tall, crouch down.)

Find with me! (Put your hand to your brow as if looking for something.)

*Where's the **slide**,* (Make a questioning gesture.)

slide, slide? (Make your hand go down an imaginary slide.)

*Find the **slide**,* (Questioning gesture, slide gesture.)

slide, slide! (Repeat slide gesture.)

Repeat with:

sandpit (Pretend to scoop sand and let it fall through your fingers.)

seesaw (Pretend to go up and down on a seesaw.)

swing (Pretend to ride a swing.)

bucket (Pretend to tip sand out of a bucket.)

spade (Pretend to scoop up sand with a spade.)

 You may wish to watch the vocabulary song video at this point.

Story time

Say the Story time chant *It's story time, story time, open the Big Book and look inside* and motion opening a book. Turn to the first two pages of the Unit 2 story. Say *What do we see? Oh, look! A (slide)!* Encourage pupils to repeat the words and do the actions while sitting down. After identifying all of the vocabulary words, close the book.

Table time

Say the Table time chant (see page 11).

Pupil's Book Page 21. Worksheet 1: Look, say and colour.

Have pupils open their books to page 21 to look at the same picture as you have opened in the Big Book. Say *Can you find this picture?* Walk around the class to help pupils find the correct page.

Have Greenman say *I want to play! But … where's the slide?* Show pupils the flashcard for the slide and have them point to it in their books and say the word. Model repeating each word, as Greenman asks about each playground item. Greenman says *Oh, thank you!* each time he finds what he is looking for with the pupils' help.

Play *The playground* song (Track 19) again for the class. Model how to point to each item in the picture while listening to the song. Repeat the song until most pupils are finding the objects.

Have Greenman say *Oh no! Your pictures need colour! Take out your pencils.* Make sure each pupil has yellow, red, light blue, dark blue, light green and dark green pencils or crayons. Have pupils complete each picture while you do the action. Take turns repeating the words with Greenman. Talk about the colours in the picture.

Sing *The playground* song again. Have pupils point to the item in the book and then do the action. While they do this, walk around the room.

Goodbye

Follow the description on page 9.

Follow the description on page 9.

Extra activities

Pupil's Book Page 22. Extra activity: Trace and colour the picture.

Say *Point to the slide.* Point to the slide in your book and monitor pupils to be sure they are pointing to the right picture. Say *Let's trace the lines with a pencil.* Model how to go over the tracing lines with a pencil to make a solid line. Repeat with each picture. Then say *Now, let's colour! Let's make the slide … yellow!* Look to see if the pupils have chosen a yellow crayon. Repeat with each picture, choosing different colours.

Game: *Point to the word*

Sing *The playground* song while playing this game. Follow the description on page 18.

Activity Book page 10 – Observe

Review the words for playground equipment and shapes.

Pupils look in the book and identify the playground equipment in the picture, then point to the shapes they can see. Pupils trace the shapes, first with their fingers, then with their pencils. Ask pupils to colour all (circles) in the picture (blue), all (squares) (red), etc.

I look carefully. Praise pupils for looking so carefully and noticing the shapes in the playground correctly. Remind pupils how important it is to take time to look around carefully and learn from their surroundings. Pupils repeat the affirmation *I look carefully* with you.

Now you! Pupils look for shapes in their own playground, and in other places around the school.

Help pupils understand the value and benefits of playing outside in the fresh air. Talk about how it helps them explore and learn about their world, as well as making their arms and legs stronger. Point out that breathing fresh oxygen into our bodies helps us to feel better.

Lesson 2

Lesson objective
To present the key structures for the unit.

Language
New: *Let's play on the (swing). Where's (the seesaw/ Greenman)?* playground items
Review: colours
Receptive: *Follow me. Let's follow the line.*

Materials
Presentation Plus, Greenman Puppet, Big Book story Unit 2, PB page 23, Flashcards Unit 2, Class Audio, sticky tape/tack, 6 (or more) pictures of Greenman's honey pot, crayons, pencils. Optional: PB page 24, Teacher Resources Worksheet 5, AB page 11

 Use Presentation Plus to watch the story video. ▷

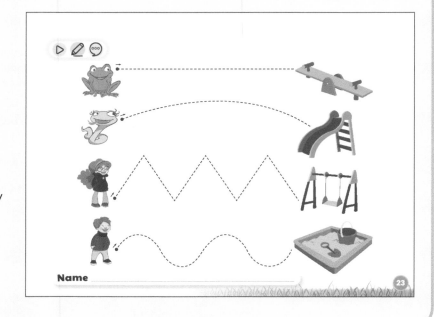

🍃 Starting the lesson

Settle the class with an opening routine (see Teacher's Book pages 8 and 9).

🍃 Active time

Warmer

Place the Unit 2 Flashcards on different walls around the classroom, in advance. Have Greenman ask *Where's the (slide)?* Have him look around the room for the flashcard of the slide. Point it out to the pupils. Repeat this process with the other five vocabulary words. Then have pupils repeat the question.

Game: *Find the honey!*

Photocopy six pictures of Greenman's honey pot and place them under the flashcards of playground items that you have placed around the room. (Or you may wish to hide enough copies so that each pupil can find one.) Take the class and Greenman to look for his honey. As you go around the room, with the pupils following you, act as if you are playing on/with the playground item represented on each card. Say *Follow me to look for Greenman's honey. Follow me to the (slide). Look! Greenman's honey! Now, follow me to the (sandpit). Look, more honey!* Continue until you have found the six (or more) honey pots.

To play this game outdoors, you could hide the honey pots under/ in actual playground objects, rather than under the flashcards.

Game: *Hide and seek*

This game can be played as a continuation of the previous game. Follow the description on page 18.

🍃 Story time

Say the Story time chant *It's story time, story time, open the Big Book and look inside* and motion opening a book. Open the Big Book to the Unit 2 story The honey game.

Elicit vocabulary learned in the previous lesson using the first pages of the story. Greenman can ask *What's this?* Model answers for the pupils to repeat. Ask about the people and things on the page. Identify the characters: Frog, Stella, Sam and Nico. Say *Where's Greenman's honey?* Greenman says *Here it is! My honey! I like honey! But oh no ... look at this honey pot! What happened?* Point to Greenman and the honey pot to give pupils an idea of what the story will be about.

Read the story or play the audio version (Track 20), pausing to use facial and hand gestures to help convey meaning.

▷ Alternatively, you may want to play the story video.

The honey game

Sam, Nico and Greenman are in the forest.
'Greenman! Let's play on the swing!' says Sam.
'Greenman! Let's play on the seesaw!' says Frog.
'Greenman! Let's play in the sandpit!' says Nico.
'Greenman! Let's play on the slide!' says Stella.
'No, thanks,' says Greenman.
'Oh, no! There's no honey!'

'Hello, Greenman. Let's play!' says Frog.
'Hello, Frog. No, thanks. Yummy, there's honey!'
'Let's follow the honey up, up, up the tree,'
says Frog. *'Let's use the seesaw.'*
'Good idea!'
'Jump up and down like me!'
'I'm up the tree! I'm so happy! I like the seesaw! Now, where's my honey?'

'Hello, Greenman. Let's play!' says Stella.
'Hello, Snake. No, thanks. Yummy, there's honey!'
'Let's follow the honey down, down,
down the tree,' says Stella. *'Let's use the slide.'*
'Good idea!'

'Slide down like me,' says Stella.
'I'm down the tree! I'm so happy. I like the slide.
Now, where's my honey?'

'Here's your honey!' say Sam and Nico.
'Thank you! I like honey. And I like the seesaw and
the slide!'
'Yay! Let's play!' says Sam.
'Let's play!' says Greenman.

Table time

Say the Table time chant (see page 11).

 **Pupil's Book page 23. Worksheet 2: Look, trace and say.**

Say *Where's (Frog)? Oh, thank you! Where's the (seesaw)? Let's follow the line.* Model how to follow the line with your finger. Say *Frog says, 'Let's play on the seesaw.'* Have pupils repeat after you *Let's play on the seesaw.* Say *Now, let's trace a line.* As pupils trace the line, continue saying *Let's play on the (seesaw)* like a chant or song. Repeat this process with the other playground items. Monitor pupils as they work.

When everyone has finished, ask, e.g. *Where's the (slide)?* and have pupils point to the correct picture. You could invite volunteers to take on your role.

Goodbye

Follow the description on page 9.

Extra activities

Pupil's Book page 24. Extra activity: Colour the bucket and spade.

Point to the picture and ask *What's this?* Elicit vocabulary for each item. Gesture how to colour in the spade and bucket. Say *Let's colour.* Monitor pupils while they complete the activity.

Teacher Resources Worksheet 5: Look and match.

Pass out one worksheet to each pupil. Say *Look, our friends are hiding!* Mime that you are hiding behind something, like a book. Say *Where's Sam? With the slide? No … . With the bucket? No … . With the seesaw? No … . With Greenman? Yes!* Point to each playground item as you say the word. Model how to connect a line from the picture of Sam hiding behind Greenman to the picture of Sam's whole body. Repeat the process for each character. If pupils show readiness, they can complete the activity on their own.

Pupils could act out being Nico, Stella or Frog and say *Let's play on the (slide).*

Activity Book page 11 – Practise

Remind pupils of the hide and seek game they played with Greenman. Explain that the forest animals are also hiding.

Use the pictures on the left to revise the forest animals, then ask *Where's the (rabbit)?* Pupils find and point to each animal in the main scene.

Pupils then colour the animals in the main scene. They can also add other details to the picture. For example, they could draw and hide another forest animal or draw themselves into the picture for their partner to find.

I have fun with my friends. Ask pupils if they like having fun with their friends and how having fun makes them feel. Find out if they play hide and seek with their friends and encourage pupils to tell you about the other games they enjoy playing with their friends. You can discuss this in L1, but translate some of their answers into English. Pupils repeat the affirmation *I have fun with my friends* with you.

Now you! Children can then play hide and seek outside, or in the classroom.

Help pupils understand that animals may often be hiding in nature where we can't see them. Remind them to be careful, for example, not to run and stamp through piles of leaves, as these might be a hiding place or habitat for a small animal.

Lesson ③

Lesson objective
To introduce a contrasting concept (up/down), and a value (exercising).

Language
New: *up/down;* playground items
Review: colours
Receptive: *Do what I do. Show me (up). Colour the (up) arrow (blue).*

Material
Presentation Plus, Greenman Puppet, Big Book story Unit 2, PB page 25, Flashcards Units 1 and 2, Pop-outs Unit 2, Class Audio, crayons, pencils, music. Optional: PB page 26, Teacher Resources Worksheet 6, a bottle of bubbles, AB page 12

 Use Presentation Plus to do the activity.

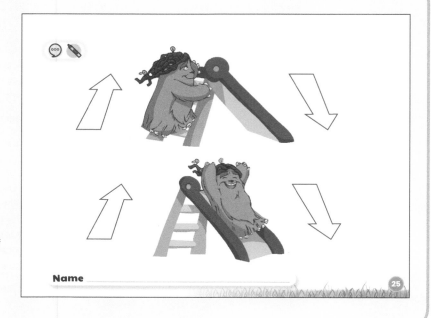

Name

🔖 Starting the lesson

Settle the class with an opening routine (see Teacher's Book pages 8 and 9).

🔖 Active time

Warmer

Review the vocabulary with the Flashcards from Units 1 and 2. Hold up flashcards and have the pupils do the action for each one.

Game: *Copy cat*

Say *Copy cat, copy cat look at me. Do what I do one, two, three! Jump up/jump down.* Then play lively music and do actions to the music. Repeat with: *Raise your leg/arm up. Put your leg/arm down.*

Game: *Up and down*

In this game, pupils will try to say *up* or *down* as quickly as they can after you surprise them with Greenman who is facing up or down. Hide Greenman behind your back and bring him out quickly with his head up (with your hand facing up). Say *What's this?* Elicit the response *Up!* Repeat the same process but with your hand (and the puppet) facing down. Say *What's this?* Elicit the response *Down!* Repeat, going quicker each time. Surprise the pupils with the order, so they have to pay close attention.

🔖 Story time

Say the Story time chant *It's story time, story time, open the Big Book and look inside* and motion opening a book.

Take out the Big Book to show the parts of the story where we can see Greenman and the children going *up* and *down*. Say *Sam goes up on the swing. Stella and Greenman go down the slide. Frog and Greenman jump up and down on the seesaw.* Pause before saying the word *up* or *down* to give pupils a chance to say the word. Say *They are exercising. They are strong!* Jog on the spot like you are exercising and make a muscle with your arm to show 'strong'.

Review the unit vocabulary using the Big Book. Ask *Where's the seesaw? What's this? It's a (slide).* You may call on individual pupils to come up and point things out in the book. Allow pupils to point rather than say the word if they are shy.

Reread the story or listen to the audio (Track 20).

▷ You may also choose to use the video for the story, pausing the video rather than pointing to pictures

🔖 Table time

Say the Table time chant (see page 11).

Do the pop-out activity.

Direct pupils' attention to the sample pop-outs that you have prepared: a set of eight cards with pairs of spades, buckets, swings and seesaws. Help the pupils to say the vocabulary word as you hold up a sample card. Show the pupils that there are two of each card. Place the cards face down on a table. Turn one card over and say the word. Then choose another card and turn it over and say the word. If the cards match, say *Yes! Two (spades)!* If they don't match, turn them both over again (face down) and say, *OK, try again.* Continue this until you have matched all of the pairs. Say *Now it's your turn!*

Show pupils how to take out the pop-out pieces carefully. Monitor as they do this and help as needed.

When all the pupils have finished, say *Show me the (swing).* Model with your own pop-out. Repeat for each card. Practise this until all of the class is participating in holding up the correct cards. Then let pupils play the game in open pairs, as you monitor. Model phrases for the pupils as they play, such as *Yes, two (seesaws)!* and *OK, try again.*

Remind pupils how to put away their pop-outs (in individual envelopes or in a common place in the classroom).

📖 Pupil's Book page 25. Worksheet 3: Say and colour *up* or *down*.

Say *Find this page in your book.* Check that pupils are on the right page. Say *Show me 'up' with your fingers.* Model pointing up with your finger while saying the word. Repeat by pointing down. Point at the first picture, say *Is Greenman going up or down? Show me with your fingers.* Repeat with the second picture. Point to the first picture and say *Colour the 'up' arrow blue for Greenman.* When pupils have finished, point to the second picture and say *Colour the 'down' arrow green for Greenman.* Again, monitor pupils' work.

🐦 Goodbye

Follow the description on page 9.

🐦 Extra activities

📖 Pupil's Book page 26. Extra activity: Trace and colour the picture.

Have pupils trace the lines around the honey pot. Encourage them to say *down* and *up* while they trace. Ask *What colour is honey? Is it blue?* Help pupils to say *yellow.* Say *Let's colour it yellow.* Monitor pupils while they complete the activity.

Game: *Bubbles*

Have Greenman take out a bottle of bubbles from a hiding place. Say *Can bubbles go up and down? Let's see!* Have Greenman model saying *up* and *down* as the bubbles move to elicit these words from the pupils. Optional: practise blowing some bubbles that are *big* and *small* to incorporate these words for extra vocabulary. Say *The big bubble is going up!* etc.

Value activity: Exercising

Have the pupils stand behind their chairs and stretch up and down. Next, have them run in place for about a minute. Have them put their hand on their heart to feel it beating quickly. Say *Good! Our hearts are strong!* (show with gestures: *heart* and *strong*). Stretch again, up and down. Point to your nose and show taking a deep breath in and out. Say *I feel good and happy! Do you?* Simply nod your head, smile and give thumbs up to show that you feel good and happy, the pupils can copy your gestures.

Emotions: Feeling happy

Point to Greenman at the end of the story and ask *Is he happy or sad?* Elicit *Happy.* Model running or swimming and say *When I (run), I feel happy. When do you feel happy?* Elicit some activities that pupils do that make them feel happy in L1. Translate their ideas into simple English.

Teacher Resources Worksheet 6: Trace and colour the honey.

Pass out one worksheet to each pupil, or ask your helper. Say *Point to Greenman. Point to the honey on the slide. Oh no! The honey goes down the slide!* Mime with your hands how the honey is dripping down the slide. Say *Let's stand up and go down the slide like the honey.* Model how honey would go down the slide very slowly. Say *Go down like honey* as you wiggle down slowly to a crouching position and then stand up to repeat. Do this until all of the children are participating.

Say *Let's sit and trace the honey with a pencil.* Hold up the worksheet and show how to trace the honey line with your pencil. Then model how to colour it with a yellow crayon. Monitor pupils as they work and offer encouragement.

📖✏️ Activity Book page 12 – Investigate

Review words for playground equipment and toys, in particular *ball* and *slide*. Make a slide by propping up a hardback book and roll a ball or another toy down it to revise *up* and *down*.

If you or your school has a marble run, you can use this to introduce the concept or show a photo or a video of how a marble run works.

Pupils then look at the children in the book who are making a marble run in the forest. Have them trace the path down the marble run, first with their finger, then with their pencils. They say *up* and *down*, as they follow the run.

🙌 **I am clever.** Praise pupils for tracing the path and remind them how clever they are for tracing the line from top to bottom correctly. Pupils repeat the affirmation *I am clever* with you.

😊 **Now you!** Pupils can construct their own marble run, or ramps, either in the class or outside. Pupils can roll different toys down their marble run and also investigate the different speeds the objects move down a slope if it's steeper or shallower.

🌱 Point out (in L1) that the children in the book are reusing tree guards to make their marble run, and that it's good to reuse objects, rather than throw things away.

Lesson 4

Lesson objective
To use TPR to review unit vocabulary through an action song.

Language
New: *Go up/down (the slide). Put your hands up/down. pick up, fill up;* playground items
Review: colours
Receptive: *turn around, wiggle; Circle it!*

Materials
Presentation Plus, Greenman Puppet, PB page 27, Flashcards Unit 2, Class Audio, pencil, crayons.
Optional: PB page 28, AB page 13

 Use Presentation Plus to watch the action song video. ▷

Name

27

🔊 Starting the lesson

Settle the class with an opening routine (see Teacher's Book pages 8 and 9).

🔊 Active time

Warmer

Do the actions for each vocabulary word for Unit 2 and have the pupils say them.

Game: *Greenman says*

Use Unit 2 vocabulary to play this version of 'Simon Says', using Greenman in place of Simon. For example, say *Greenman says: Go up on the seesaw.* The pupils pretend to go up and down on the imaginary seesaw, but only when they hear 'Greenman says' before the instruction. Be sure to keep the game fun and not competitive and encourage pupils to say *Well done!* to children who do well in the game.

Up and down action song: Watch the video. Sing and do the actions.

 You may prefer to use the action song video to teach the pupils the actions and the song.

First, play the audio and hold up flashcards for the vocabulary words in the song. Invite the pupils to say the word when you hold up the card. The second time you play the song, do the actions to show the class. Next, have the pupils stand up *(Stand up, stand up, 1–2–3. Stand up, stand up tall with me).* Teach them the actions one by one as you say each line of the song.

Practise the actions for the song three or four times slowly, going through the song line by line. Then, play the audio track and do the actions together. Repeat until all of the class is participating in each action and singing some of the words.

🎧 21 Up and down 🎵

Put your hands up, put your hands down.
(Raise your hands, put them down.)

Give a little wiggle, wiggle, wiggle, wiggle and turn around! (Shake your hips, turn around in a circle.)

Go up the slide, go down the slide. (Climb an imaginary ladder, go down an imaginary slide.)

Give a little wiggle, wiggle, wiggle, wiggle and turn around. (Shake your hips, turn around in a circle.)

Repeat with:

Go up on the seesaw, go down on the seesaw.
(Go up on your toes holding on to an imaginary seesaw handle in front of you, bend your knees low holding onto the imaginary seesaw handle.)

Go up on the swing, go down on the swing.
(Hold imaginary swing ropes at your sides and swing up to your tiptoes, hold imaginary swing ropes and swing down and bend your knees.)

Run up the sandpit, run down the sandpit.
(Run in place going up on your tiptoes, run in place bending your knees.)

Fill up the bucket, put down the bucket.
(Pick up an imaginary bucket from the floor with two hands, put the imaginary bucket down on the floor with two hands.)

Pick up the spade, put down the spade.
(Pretend to scoop sand into an imaginary bucket, put the imaginary spade down on the floor.)

🍃 Table time

Say the Table time chant (see page 11).

📓 Pupils Book page 27. Worksheet 4: Look and circle the actions in the song.

Show pupils page 27 in your Pupil's Book and check that everyone has the correct page and their pencils ready. Pupils will listen to the *Up and down* action song (Track 21) again and circle the actions that appear in the song.

Demonstrate how to act out each of the actions shown on the page for the pupils to join in, while seated. Say *Point to the action in the song.* Play the *Up and down* action song, and model pointing to the pictures of actions from the song. Some pupils will notice that there are two activities that are not in the song. Say and point to the pictures *Go down the slide, yes! Circle it!* (Model circling the picture with your finger and monitor pupils as they circle in their books.) *Open the window?* (long pause) *No, no, no! It doesn't go here, no circle!* (Shake your head and exaggerate the no.) *Give a little wiggle, yes! Circle it! Close the door?* (long pause) *No, no, no! No circle, it doesn't go here! Put your hands up, yes! Circle it!*

🍃 Goodbye

Follow the description on page 9.

🍃 Extra activities

📓 Pupil's Book page 28. Extra activity: Draw and colour your favourite playground activity.

Use flashcards to help pupils to think about their favourite playground activity. Ask questions to give ideas. *Do you like to play in the sandpit? Do you like to go down the slide?* Monitor pupils while they work, and ask questions about their pictures. You may choose to have pupils share their pictures with their partners or with the class and use the phrase *I like the (slide).*

Game: *What am I playing with?*

Act out using a playground item for the class and say *What's this?* If no one responds, say the answer for the class to repeat. Show a volunteer a flashcard and have them act out the item for the class to guess. If the class doesn't guess the word, say it for them to repeat.

 **Activity Book page 13 – Find and make**

Pupils find natural materials and use them to decorate a sandcastle. They can find the natural materials outside, either before or during the lesson. Alternatively, bring the materials to class for pupils to find. As well as the natural materials pupils find (stones, leaves, feathers, flowers and pinecones or acorns), you will also need to provide wet sand in a sandpit or tray, and buckets and spades.

Review the words *sand*, *bucket* and *spade*. Show or draw a picture of a sandcastle to pre-teach the word.

Use the individual pictures in the book to describe the different natural materials in English and L1. Point to the sandcastle in the book and tell pupils they are going to make one and decorate it with the natural materials. Direct pupils' attention to how the materials are used in the example in the book.

Pupils look for the natural materials, either outside or among the materials that have been brought to the classroom. When they find one of the items in the pictures, they can circle it.

🙂 **Now you!** Pupils take turns to make and decorate sandcastles. They can work in pairs, or as a class to make a sand city. They can look at the different sandcastles and compare the designs.

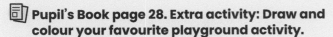 **I am creative.** Compare pupils' ideas for their sand castles and say *Well done! You are creative.* Encourage pupils to repeat the affirmation *I am creative* with you.

🌱 Help pupils learn about animals that live in sand, for example sand worms, or about animals that lay their eggs in sand, for example turtles.

Lesson 5

Lesson objective
To work on pre-writing skills and practise numbers through a song.

Language
New: playground items
Review: colours; shapes; numbers *1–4*
Receptive: *Where's something (red)? Let's (clap).*
It's your turn. Draw another (swing).

Materials
Presentation Plus, Greenman Puppet, PB page 29, Class Audio, pencil, crayons. Optional: PB page 30, Teacher Resources Worksheet 7, AB page 14

 Use Presentation Plus to do the activities.

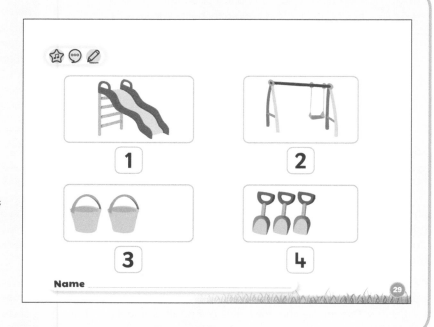

🍃 Starting the lesson

Settle the class with an opening routine (see Teacher's Book pages 8 and 9).

🍃 Active time

Warmer

Review colours, shapes and numbers *1–4*. After reviewing all of the colours, look for things in the classroom that are that colour. Say *Where's something red? The book is red!* Let the children look for other examples. For shapes, say *Where's something square? The boxes are squares!* For numbers, say *Where's something with two? I've got two eyes, one, two!*

Game: *Count and clap*

Practise saying numbers and having the pupils count that number of times. Say *Let's clap one time, one* (clap once) *two* (clap twice). Continue to *four*. To begin with, clap along with the pupils. Once they are more confident in the activity, they can clap on their own. Continue the activity, saying the numbers in random order. Then say *(Lucía), it's your turn.* Model what to do, quietly if necessary, for the pupil to copy. Say the number along with the pupils. Continue until everyone has had a turn.

Count and clap number song 1–4: Sing and count.

Say *We know our numbers very well! Let's practise a song with them.* Have the pupils sit or stand and tell them to listen for the claps. Model saying *one*, and clapping once, *two*, and clapping twice, etc.

Play the song, clapping along as you count.

🎧 **22** **Count and clap** 🎵

1, 2, 3, 4!
1, 2, 3, 4!
Count and clap, really slow.
Everyone, here we go!

1! Clap!
2! Clap! Clap!
3! Clap! Clap! Clap!
4! Clap! Clap! Clap! Clap!
1, 2, 3, 4!
1, 2, 3, 4!

 Table time

Say the Table time chant (see page 11).

📖 Pupil's Book page 29. Worksheet 5: Count and draw what's missing.

Call pupils' attention to the Pupil's Book. Check to make sure everyone is on the correct page. Say *Let's count the playground items.* Point to the first picture and have Greenman say *Look, one slide. One, is that correct? Yes, one. Now, here are two swings.* (show two fingers to emphasise) *Two, right?* Act as if you are going to carry on and wait for pupils to correct you. Greenman says *Oh no! We need to draw another swing. Draw another swing, the number is two!* Repeat the same process with the pictures of the buckets and the spades. (Pupils must draw one missing bucket and one missing spade.)

Goodbye

Follow the description on page 9.

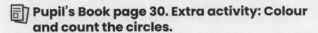 Extra activities

📖 Pupil's Book page 30. Extra activity: Colour and count the circles.

Hold up page 30 in the Pupil's Book and check that the pupils are on the correct page. Help pupils to prepare the crayons that they will need (blue, green, red, and yellow). Point to the first honey lid, and say *Colour this blue.* Monitor children as they find the right colour and colour in the lid. Repeat the process with the other lids in different colours. Then have pupils count the lids together.

Teacher Resources Worksheet 7: Help Greenman find the honey.

Pass out one worksheet for each pupil, or ask your helper. Say *Oh no, Greenman has lost his honey again! Can you help him?* Use gestures to show tracing the dashed line with your finger. Say *Use your pencil to find the honey.* Monitor pupils as they work and help as needed.

📝 Activity Book page 14 – Feel

Pupils do some simple exercises with you in class – stretching up, touching their toes, walking, running and jumping on the spot, etc. As you do each one, say: *That feels good. I feel happy. Exercising is fun!*

Pupils look at the picture in the book. Explain that the children are going for a walk out in the country, and doing different activities and exercises outside.

Show pupils how to trace the children's route, first with their finger, then with their pencil.

Ask pupils to decide which of the activities in the picture they like doing. They colour in the children who are about to do these activities.

🙂 **Now you!** Pupils can then go outside to do some exercise in the playground. Alternatively, repeat a simple exercise routine inside.

🧘 **I feel happy.** After you have done some exercise together, smile and say *I feel happy.* Ask pupils if they feel happy too, and remind them that we often feel happy when we take exercise and have fun. Pupils repeat the affirmation *I feel happy* with you.

🌱 Help pupils to appreciate the natural opportunities the outdoors gives us for taking exercise in different ways – walking, climbing, rolling, running and jumping.

Lesson 6

Lesson objective
To consolidate all unit content.

Language
Review: playground items; Big Book language structures
Receptive: *Is it a (slide)? Find and stick.*

Materials
Presentation Plus, Greenman Puppet, PB page 31, Flashcards Units 1 and 2, Class Audio, Stickers Unit 2, pencil, crayons. Optional: AB page 15

 Use Presentation Plus to play the games.

Consolidation

WORKSHEET 6

Find, stick and say.

Name _____

31

Starting the lesson

Settle the class with an opening routine (see Teacher's Book pages 8 and 9).

Active time

Warmer

Review Flashcards from Units 1 and 2 by holding each one up and saying the word with the pupils. You may wish to use the audio of the Unit 2 vocabulary to review (Track 18).

Game: *Flashcard on my head*

Give a pupil a 'secret' flashcard to hold on his/her head without looking at it. The pupil has to try to guess the word by using the phrase *Is it a (slide)?* The other pupils will respond *yes* or *no* until the correct vocabulary word is guessed. If the pupil struggles, use gestures and clues to help him/her feel comfortable and reach the correct answer. Repeat with different pupils until you have reviewed all the vocabulary from Units 1 and 2.

Story review

Say the Story time chant (see page 10) and motion opening a book. Reread the story, inviting the pupils to participate in saying the words or lines that they know.

▷ Alternatively, you may want to play the story video.

Table time

Say the Table time chant (see page 11).

Pupil's Book page 31. Worksheet 6: Find, stick and say.

Help the pupils to find page 31 in the Pupil's Book and locate the stickers for Unit 2. Say *Find and stick the pictures.* Have Greenman repeat each word several times as pupils look for the correct

sticker to put in each place. Monitor pupils as they work and encourage them along, or give gesture clues. Repeat with each vocabulary word. When they have finished, have pupils point to the stickers and say the words.

Goodbye

Follow the description on page 9.

Activity Book page 15 – Care

Introduce the idea of drawing in the sand by showing photos of different kinds of sand art – drawings, collages or sculptures. Pupils can say which their favourite is.

Pupils look at the picture in the book and draw their face on the child by the sandpit. Point to the very happy boy and ask *Is he happy or sad ? (Happy).* Then explain that they have made him happy by making something for him in the sand. Ask pupils to imagine what they made. Help them to share their ideas, then they draw and colour what they imagined. Pupils can share their pictures.

I am kind. Point to the very happy boy and ellicit why he is happy (his friend has drawn a picture/made a sculpture for him in the sand). Remind pupils that it's kind to help our friends and to try to make them feel happy. Encourage pupils to repeat the affirmation *I am kind* with you.

☺ **Now you!** If you have a sandpit or sand tray, pupils can make some sand art themselves. Alternatively, they can draw a picture for a friend on paper.

🌱 Help pupils appreciate that playing together outside makes us feel happy and that they can have fun in nature in different ways.

To end the unit, pupils circle the frog on page 2.

Extra Phonics Lesson

Lesson objective
To introduce two new phonics sounds ('i' and 'o').

Language
New: *in, on*

Materials
Presentation Plus, Greenman Puppet, PB page 32, downloadable Phonics Flashcards, Class Audio, a ball, a box, crayons, pencils. Optional: Teacher Resources Worksheet 8, scissors

📎 Phonics time

Warmer

Show children the *i* (in) and *o* (on) Phonics Flashcards. Read the words then segment the sounds. Say *Look at the picture: There is a ball in the jar. Listen to the sound: i. Listen and repeat: i-i-i-i-nnn.* Repeat with the second sound.

Point to the Phonics Flashcards and have pupils segment the different sounds three times.

📖 Pupil's Book page 32. 1. Listen and say the *i* and *o* letter sounds.

Have Greenman use a small ball to show *in* and *on* with different things in the class (a box, a cupboard, etc.). Greenman models the target phonics sound before saying the whole word *i-i-i-in, o-o-o-on.* Pupils repeat in the same manner. Have pupils open their books to page 32. Say *Point to 'in'. Say i-i-i-in.* while pointing to the picture. Repeat for *on*. Play the audio and have pupils listen and repeat the sounds and words three times.

 23

i – i – i	*in*
o – o – o	*on*

📖 Pupil's Book page 32. 2. Sing the song.

Show pupils the picture in activity 2. Play the song and have pupils follow the path of the butterfly in the picture. After playing the track three times, say it slowly and have the pupils repeat each line while following the butterfly with a finger. Repeat (in different voices or have Greenman speak, to hold interest). Continue repeating until pupils are saying at least the *in* and *on* parts of the song.

 24

In – on; in – on.
This is my song!

In – on; in – on.
This is my song!

I'm in the forest,
I'm in the tree,
I'm on the rose,
I'm in Sam's hand,
And I'm on Nico's nose!

📖 Pupil's Book page 32. 3. Listen, point and say.

Show pupils activity 3 in your book. Play the audio for the first picture and pause. Show the flashcard to reinforce the word. Encourage the pupils to say the word out loud as they point. Pause the audio throughout the track to give plenty of time for reinforcing the information with gestures or flashcards, as pupils point and say.

 25

i	*in*	*a cat in a box*
o	*on*	*a rabbit on a book*
o	*on*	*a frog on a box*
i	*in*	*a dog in a bag*
o	*on*	*a rabbit on a table*

📎 Extra activities

Teacher Resources Worksheet 8: Trace and cut out the insect and the orange.

Prepare one worksheet for each pupil in advance. Review the *i* and the *o* sounds with the class. Model tracing the line inside the insect's body and the *i* below, and say *i i i insect.* Have the pupils do the same and repeat the word. Repeat with *orange* and the letter *o*. When the pupils have finished tracing, have them cut out the pictures and use them to play a game. Give an instruction like *The insect is on your head.* Model holding the insect picture on your head and gesture for the pupils to do the same. Repeat with various instructions.

Autumn fun

Lesson objective
To review vocabulary from Units 1 and 2 and sing a song about autumn.

Language
New: *leaves; brown*
Review: *red, yellow; cloudy, cold, rainy, windy;* classroom and playground items
Receptive: *blow, move; Let's draw a line.*

Materials
Presentation Plus, Greenman Puppet, PB page 33, Flashcards Units 1 and 2, Class Audio, autumn leaves, crayons, pencils. Optional: PB page 34, Teacher Resources Worksheets 9 and 10, paints, glue sticks, scissors

🍂 Starting the lesson

Settle the class with an opening routine (see Teacher's Book pages 8 and 9).

🍂 Active time

Warmer

Review weather vocabulary (you can use the Routine Boards on Presentation Plus to do this). Pupils can choose the vocabulary that is most appropriate for autumn. Have the pupils use gestures to show the different types of weather. (Show rain falling with your fingers, blow out air and move your hands in swirling motions for *windy*, and shiver, saying *brrr* to show *cold*.)

Say the vocabulary.

Have Greenman hold up each of the Flashcards from Units 1 and 2. The pupils say (or repeat) each word. Then, speed up to have pupils try to identify the words as quickly as possible.

Autumn leaves song: Sing and do the actions.

Show the pupils the leaves that you have brought to class (real or artificial). Talk about the colours and teach *brown*. Say *How do leaves move?* Drop one of the leaves from up high and say *Move down, move down, move down* as the leaf drops. Hold another leaf in your hand and say *The wind blows them round and round.* Pretend to blow the leaf round like you are the wind. Have the pupils join in.

Play the song once and model the actions. Then have the pupils join in as you say the song line by line and do the actions with them. Repeat this until most pupils are saying some of the words and participating in the actions. Then play the audio again, modelling the actions with the pupils participating. Repeat the song until the class is singing most of the words and doing the actions.

 Autumn leaves

Autumn leaves are red and brown. (Twist your wrists back and forth like a falling leaf.)

Autumn winds blow them round. (Move your hands back and forth in front of you like they are blowing in the wind.)

Cold and windy. Cold and windy. (Wrap your arms around you like you are cold, move your body from side to side like it's blowing in the wind.)

Autumn leaves move up and down. (Put your hands up over your head, crouch down and touch the floor.)

Autumn leaves are yellow and brown. (Twist your wrists back and forth like a falling leaf.)

Autumn rains wash them round. (Wiggle your fingers to make 'rain' then move your 'rainy' fingers round in front of you.)

Cloudy, rainy. Cloudy, rainy. (Hold palms above your head parallel to the floor and 'bounce' them for 'cloudy', wiggle your fingers to make 'rain'.)

Autumn leaves move up and down. (Put your hands up over your head, crouch down and touch the floor.)

🍃 Table time

Say the Table time chant (see page 11).

📖 Pupil's Book page 33. Worksheet 1: Look, match and say.

Show pupils page 33 and walk around to check that everyone is on the correct page.

Say *Where's the classroom?* Show pupils how to point to the school photo. Say *Where's the playground?* Show pupils how to point to the playground photo. Say *Where does the window go? Let's draw a line.* Model how to draw a line from the window to the classroom. Repeat the process with the other pictures, matching the items to either the photo of the classroom or the playground. Pupils may be able to work independently on this. Review the activity as a class, saying *What's in the (classroom)?* Have pupils say the correct answers together.

🍃 Goodbye

Follow the description on page 9.

🍃 Extra activities

📖 Pupil's Book page 34. Extra activity: Trace and colour the leaves.

Show the pupils one of the leaves that you have brought to class. Draw their attention to the veins on the leaf. Trace them with your finger, or have a pupil come up to trace them.

Now direct their attention to page 34. Say *Let's trace the lines on the leaf with a pencil.* Model how to do this in your book. Monitor as pupils work. Then repeat with the second leaf. When pupils have finished tracing, they may colour the leaves in the autumn colours that you have talked about. You may also choose to sing the *Autumn leaves* song (Track 26).

Game: *Pass, stop and say*

Use Flashcards from Units 1 and 2 to play this game. Follow the description on page 18.

Teacher Resources Worksheets 9 and 10: Paint, cut and stick to make a tree.

Prepare the autumn project worksheets for each pupil in advance. Play the song, *Autumn leaves* (Track 26), again. Hold up the autumn scene worksheet and say *Let's make an autumn tree!* Have pupils paint or colour Worksheet 9. Show the pupils Worksheet 10. Say *Point to the leaves.* Model how to point to each leaf. Say *Let's paint the leaves with autumn colours.* Model painting a leaf (green, brown, red, or yellow). Have pupils paint their leaves in different autumn colours. Model cutting out the pictures. When the pupils have cut out their leaves, say *Now, let's stick our leaves onto the tree.* Let the pupils stick the leaves wherever they want. After the pupils have finished, say *Now let's make it a windy, rainy day.* Have pupils identify the windy and rainy clouds (you can do actions to help them), then have them cut out their clouds. Model how to stick the clouds near the tree. Make an autumn display with the worksheets.

Unit 3: I'm hurt!

Lesson 1

Lesson objective
To introduce the main vocabulary for the unit (the body).

Language
New: *arm, finger, foot, hand, leg, tummy; black, brown, white*
Review: *colours*
Receptive: *touch; What is it? What colour is this? Where's (Greenman's arm)? Let's circle it with (brown).*

Materials
Presentation Plus, Greenman Puppet, Big Book story Unit 3, PB page 35, Flashcards Units 1, 2 and 3, Class Audio, pencils. Optional: PB page 36, AB page 16

 Use Presentation Plus to watch the unit introduction video and vocabulary song video. ▷

🔊 Starting the lesson

Settle the class with an opening routine (see Teacher's Book pages 8 and 9).

🔊 Active time

Welcome to Unit 3

▷ Tell pupils that you are about to start a new unit. Play the Unit 3 introduction video to introduce the unit topic. Pause the video at different points and ask, in L1, what the children can see and what they think they will learn about in this unit.

Warmer

Have Greenman take out the Units 1 and 2 Flashcards. Help the children do the motions/gestures and say the words.

Game: *Run to the word*

Greenman will take out the Unit 3 Flashcards. Act very excited about the new words. Take each flashcard out individually and say *Look! Arm! Repeat class, 'arm'! What is it? (Arm!)* While you say the word, use gestures to reinforce the concept. Repeat this process with each card.

See page 19 for a description of the game.

At this point, you may wish to use the audio of the unit vocabulary to listen and repeat as a class.

🎧 **27** *arm, finger, foot, hand, leg, tummy*

My body rap: Rap and touch

Say the Stand up chant *Stand up, stand up, 1–2–3. Stand up, stand up tall with me!*

Play the *My body* rap. Hold up the corresponding flashcard when you hear each vocabulary word in the rap. Play the audio while pointing to the different parts of the body. Encourage pupils to touch their body while they listen. Next, say the rap line by line, slowly, enunciating the words for pupils to repeat. Play the audio again and repeat the rap three times, or until most pupils are touching the correct parts of their body and saying some of the words.

🎧 **28** **My body**

Hello everyone.
Let's do the body rap!
Are you ready?
Let's start!

*Where's your **hand**?*
Hand, hand.
*Touch your **hand**!*
Hand, hand.
And now it's time for ...

Repeat with: *leg, arm, finger, tummy, foot*

▷ You may wish to watch the vocabulary song video at this point.

📖 Story time

Say the Story time chant *It's story time, story time, open the Big Book and look inside* and motion opening a book. Open the Big Book to the first two pages of the Unit 3 story. Say *What do we see? Oh, look! (Arm!)* Encourage pupils to repeat the words and point to the parts of the body. Direct pupils' attention to the items in the picture that are white, brown or black to present these colours. Say *It's windy. Look at Sam's scarf. It's white. Look at Nico's hat. It's black. Look at the leaves. They're brown.* After identifying all of the vocabulary words, close the book.

📖 Table time

Say the Table time chant (see page 11).

📘 Pupil's Book page 35. Worksheet 1: Look, circle and say the parts of the body.

Show pupils page 35 and walk around to check that everyone is on the correct page.

Play the *My body* rap (Track 28) again. Model how to point to each item in the picture while listening to the song.

Point to each of the circles around Greenman, Sam and Nico and ask *What colour is this? (Brown, red, black.)* Have Greenman say *Take out your crayons.* Say *Where's Greenman's arm? Is it this?* Point to the leg. Elicit the response *No.* You may add *No, it's a (leg)!* Repeat with the other parts of the body shown. When you get to Greenman's arm, say *Here! Greenman's arm! Let's circle it with brown! Show me a brown crayon.* Have pupils hold up the correct colour crayon. Repeat this process with the parts of the body for the other characters, using red for Sam and black for Nico. (Pupils circle Greenman's tummy with brown, Sam's finger and hand with red and Nico's leg and foot with black).

Sing the *My body* rap again. Have pupils point to each item in the book and then point to that part on their own body.

📖 Goodbye

Follow the description on page 9.

📖 Extra activities

📘 Pupil's Book page 36. Extra activity: Draw and colour Sam or Nico.

Show the pupils pages 18 and 19 in the Big Book and direct their attention to the pictures of Sam and Nico. Draw a simple version of one of them on the board. Have pupils choose either Sam or Nico to draw in their Pupil's Books. Have them colour their drawings and talk about the colours they are using for the characters' clothes.

Look and do.

The pupils will copy your motions while you chant the vocabulary word. Say *Do what I do.* Raise your arm and encourage pupils to raise their arms. Say *Arm, arm, arm, arm.* Repeat with the other parts of the body. Optional: choose a volunteer to model the motions.

📒 Activity Book page 16 – Observe

Introduce the word *cloud* by drawing a cloud on the board, or pointing to a cloud in the sky.

Use the pictures on the page to introduce the idea of seeing images in clouds.

Pupils guess the images in the clouds on the page – first orally. You may wish to teach a mime for each cloud, as well as point to the pictures.

Check understanding by pointing to the clouds. Pupils do the mime for a rabbit, a child running or a teddy.

Pupils match the clouds to the pictures, first with their fingers, then with a pencil.

🙌 **I use my imagination.** Check the activity and praise pupils (in L1) for using their imagination to see the pictures in the clouds. Pupils repeat the affirmation *I use my imagination* with you.

☺ **Now you!** Pupils can go out into the playground to find clouds to look at. If there aren't any clouds in the sky, you could do a similar activity, looking at trees and tree stump shapes.

🌱 Help pupils notice the different colours in clouds. Explain that black or grey clouds are full of water vapour for rain.

Lesson ②

Lesson objective
To present the key structure for the unit.

Language
New: *What's the matter? My (leg) hurts. Yes, I can.*
the body
Review: *up/down, happy/sad;* colours; numbers 1–4
Receptive: *number 5; Pass the ball. Stop! Can you move your (fingers)? What's this? Be careful! Circle the (sad) face.*

Materials
Presentation Plus, Greenman Puppet, Big Book story Unit 3, PB page 37, Flashcards Unit 3, Class Audio, soft ball, music, crayons, pencils. Optional: PB page 38, Teacher Resources Worksheet 11, scissors, glue sticks, AB page 17

 Use Presentation Plus to watch the story video. ▷

🍃 Starting the lesson

Settle the class with an opening routine (see Teacher's Book pages 8 and 9).

🍃 Active time

Warmer

Review the vocabulary using the Unit 3 Flashcards.

Game: *Pass the ball*

Have pupils sit in a circle. Take out a soft ball from a hiding place. Place the unit flashcards in the centre of the circle, face down. Say *Let's play a game. Let's pass the ball.* Pass the ball to your right and motion for the pupils to continue doing the same. When the ball returns to you, say *Stop!* Pick up a flashcard from the centre, turn it over and say the word. Say *Now you!* Repeat the same process but this time stop on a pupil. Help the pupil to choose a card and say the word (help if he/she finds the word difficult). Practise one more time in the same way. Next, turn on lively music as the pupils pass the ball, and stop the music when you say *Stop!* Repeat until all the pupils have had a turn.

Listen and do.

Say *Can you move your (fingers)?* Wiggle your own fingers and model the response *Yes, I can.* Repeat with other parts of the body. You can exaggerate the gestures for 'move' to explain the verb. Optional: have a pupil, or pupils, lead the activity.

🍃 Story time

Say the Story time chant *It's story time, story time, open the Big Book and look inside* and motion opening a book.

Open the Big Book to the Unit 3 story *I'm hurt!* Look at the first page of the story and elicit vocabulary learned in the previous lesson. Have Greenman ask *What's this?* Point to different parts of the body, model answers for the pupils to repeat. Ask about the people and things on the page, pointing out the black, white and brown objects as well. Turn to the first page of the story text. Say *Look, Sam is going up and down.* Greenman says *Yes, up and down! But be careful!*

Read the story or play the audio version (Track 29), pausing to use facial and hand gestures to help convey meaning.

▷ Alternatively, you may want to play the story video.

 I'm hurt!

Sam, Nico and Greenman are going for a walk in the forest. It's a windy day. They are very happy.
'I like the forest! I go up and down!' says Sam.
'I like the forest! I go up and down!' says Nico.
'Up, down! Up, down!'
'It's a windy day. Remember, be careful!'
says Greenman.

'Be careful!' says Greenman.
'Oh, no! I'm hurt!' says Nico.
'I can help!'
'My leg! My foot!'

'Be careful!' says Greenman.
'Oh, no! I'm hurt,' says Sam.
'I can help!'
'My hand! My finger!'

'What's the matter, Nico?' says Greenman.
'My leg hurts.'
'Can you move your leg?'
'Yes, I can.'
'Good! But your leg is dirty. Let's clean it and put on a plaster.'
'I've got a plaster!' says Sam.

'What's the matter, Sam?' says Greenman.
'My hand hurts. My finger hurts.'
'Can you move your fingers?'
'Yes, I can.'
'One, two, three, four ... four fingers! Oh, no! You are hurt!' says Greenman.

'No!' says Nico.
'One, two, three, four, five! Five fingers! Your finger is dirty!'
'Let's clean it and put on a plaster,' says Greenman.
'Remember, be careful!'

Game: *What's the matter?*

This game practises the language seen in the story. Act as if you have hurt your leg, exaggerate your facial expressions so that this is clear for the pupils. Have pupils say *What's the matter?* (You may wish to have Greenman say this for pupils to repeat the first time.) Say *My leg hurts.* Call up a volunteer to act out that they have hurt another part of the body. Model for the whole class, or one pupil, to ask *(Lucía) what's the matter?* Help the pupil to respond *My (hand) hurts.* Repeat until many of the pupils have had a turn.

🍃 Table time

Say the Table time chant (see page 11).

📑 Pupil's Book page 37. Worksheet 2: Look and circle the correct face.

Show pupils page 37 and walk around to check that everyone is on the correct page. Focus pupils' attention on the first picture by pointing to it and holding the book up. Say *Is Nico happy? No, he's sad. Now circle the sad face.* Monitor as pupils complete the activity individually, then review the answers as a class.

🍃 Goodbye

Follow the description on page 9.

🍃 Extra activities

📑 Pupil's Book page 38. Extra activity: Draw and colour yourself.

Prepare in advance an example of the activity, either drawing a picture of yourself on the board or personalising the picture on page 38 by adding your hair, glasses, etc. Show pupils your completed picture. Say *Look, it's me! Now draw you!* Monitor as pupils complete the activity and ask questions about the different parts of the body. Allow time for them to colour their pictures.

Teacher Resources Worksheet 11: Cut and stick.

Pass out the worksheet or ask your helper. Hold up a worksheet and point to the parts of the body that are featured in the smaller pictures. Say *What's this?* Elicit the vocabulary (*finger, leg, foot*). Model the activity, then let pupils work on their own to cut and stick the smaller pictures onto the characters.

Volunteers could act out being the children in the pictures, as Greenman asks them *What's the matter?*

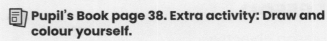

✏️ Activity Book page 17 – Find and make

Pupils find natural materials and use them to make a collage of a stick person. Pupils can find some of the natural materials outside, either before or during the lesson, or alternatively bring the materials to class for pupils to find. Pupils will need to find: a stick with a fork at the end, a straight stick, leaves, acorns or small conkers, feathers.

Use the natural materials to make a collage picture on the floor of the classroom (e.g. inside the class circle at circle time). Pupils guess what it is.

Use the individual pictures in the book to talk about the different natural materials in English and L1. Point to the natural stick person collage in the book and tell pupils they are going to make one with the natural materials. Direct pupils' attention to how the materials are used in the example in the book.

Pupils look for the natural materials, either outside or among the materials that have been brought to the classroom. When they find one of the items in the pictures, they can circle it.

☺ **Now you!** Pupils make their stick people with the materials they find.

🧘 **I am creative.** Praise pupils for their stick people. Tell pupils they are creative because they have used their ideas to each make different looking stick people. Pupils repeat the affirmation *I am creative* with you.

🌱 Encourage pupils to return any items they found outdoors after they have made their stick people – and help them understand that some of the items are seeds (acorns), or provide goodness for the soil (flowers, grass and leaves).

Lesson 3

Lesson objective
To introduce a contrasting concept (clean/dirty), and a value (being careful).

Language
New: *clean/dirty; Your/My (leg) is (dirty)! Let's clean it! What's the matter? My (leg) hurts.* the body
Review: colours
Receptive: *Show me. Let's glue the (head). Circle him/her! Don't circle him/her! Be careful!*

Materials
Presentation Plus, Greenman Puppet, Big Book story Unit 3, PB page 39, Pop-outs Unit 3, Class Audio, facecloth, glue sticks, crayons, pencils. Optional: PB page 40, Teacher Resources Worksheet 12, AB page 18

 Use Presentation Plus to do the activity.

Name _____

39

🔊 Starting the lesson

Settle the class with an opening routine (see Teacher's Book pages 8 and 9).

🔊 Active time

Warmer
Practise the game from Lesson 2 *What's the matter?* to review language.

Listen and do.
Say *Greenman is dirty! Let's clean Greenman.* Act as if you are cleaning Greenman's body, saying the parts of the body. Have pupils stand up (say the Stand up chant on page 10). Make a circular motion, as if you are including everyone and say *Let's clean our legs!* Repeat with the other vocabulary words.

🔊 Story time

Say the Story time chant *It's story time, story time, open the Big Book and look inside* and motion opening a book.

Take out the Big Book to show the parts of the story where we can see Greenman and his friends either *clean* or *dirty*. Say *Nico's leg is dirty.* Have the pupils repeat the sentence, or just the word *dirty*. Do this again with *Sam's finger is dirty.*

Review the unit vocabulary using the Big Book. You may call on individual pupils to come up and point things out in the book. Allow pupils to point rather than say the word if they are shy.

Reread the story or listen to the audio (Track 29).

▷ You may also choose to use the video for the story, pausing the video rather than pointing to pictures

Do a role-play.
Show the Big Book picture of Nico's dirty leg on page 22. Say *Nico's leg is dirty.* Scrunch up your nose, say *Is your leg dirty?* Look at your own leg and say *Oh no, my leg is dirty! Let's clean it!* Act out washing your leg with a facecloth or piece of fabric and encourage pupils to 'wash' their own leg. Then say *My leg is clean!* Call up a volunteer to say a dialogue with you. Say *Oh, your leg is dirty! Let's clean it!* Act out washing the pupil's leg. Whisper the line *Thank you. My leg is clean!* for the pupil to repeat. Call up a second volunteer, use your hands to gesture as you say *You be me.* Now, whisper the lines to each pupil for them to repeat. When this group finishes, say *Well done!* for the class to repeat. Call up two more volunteers. Whisper the lines to them if necessary and repeat the process with a different part of the body. Continue until the children are saying many lines on their own and lots, or all, of the pupils have had a chance to participate.

🔊 Table time

Say the Table time chant (see page 11).

Do the pop-out activity.
Direct pupils' attention to the sample pop-out that you have prepared: a torso onto which they can attach a head, arms and legs. Help the pupils to say the parts of the body and hold each one up as they say the words.

Show pupils how to take out the pop-out pieces carefully. Monitor as they do this and help as needed.

When all the pupils have finished, say *Show me the body.* Model holding up the pop-out. Say *Show me one arm.* Model with your own pop-out. Repeat with *Show me two arms.* Practise this with the head and legs as well. Continue until the whole class is participating in holding up their pop-outs and saying the parts of the body. Then, say *We're ready to glue. Show me the head.* (pause) *Let's glue the head.* Model how to connect the piece to the torso. Repeat the process with the other parts, or let the pupils finish on their own. When they have finished, model how to practise pointing and saying the parts of the body.

Remind pupils how to put away their pop-outs (in individual envelopes or in a common place in the classroom).

📑 Pupil's Book page 39. Worksheet 3: Say *clean* or *dirty*. Circle the dirty children.

Show pupils page 39 and walk around to check that everyone is on the correct page. Point to the picture of the child jumping in a puddle. Say *Is he clean or dirty?* The pupils will answer *Dirty.* Say *Let's circle him.* Next gesture to indicate all of the pictures and call on a pupil to come up and point out another 'dirty' child. Say *Let's circle him/her!* Point to a picture of a 'clean' child. Say *Is he/she dirty?* Pause for them to answer *No! He's/She's clean!* Say *Don't circle him/her!* Motion for 'don't circle', shake your finger 'no'. Continue the process until the pupils have completed the activity.

🍃 Goodbye

Follow the description on page 9.

🍃 Extra activities

📑 Pupil's Book page 40. Extra activity: Trace and colour the picture.

The pupils will trace and colour the lines of the water to help the boy wash his hands. Say *We need water to wash.* Do actions for turning on a tap and washing your hands; have the pupils do the same. Next, hold up your book and show how to colour in the water, first with your finger, then with a blue crayon. When the pupils have finished, say *Now, colour the picture.* Monitor as pupils complete the activity.

Game: *Let's clean it!*

Review classroom and body vocabulary with the contrasting concept clean/dirty. Greenman says *Oh no! The (chair) is dirty!* Say *Let's clean it!* Take out a facecloth from a hiding place or from your pocket and wipe the chair quickly. Greenman says *Now the (chair) is clean!* Greenman says *Oh no! My (hand) is dirty!* Say *Let's clean it!* Use the facecloth to clean Greenman's hand. Then Greenman says *Now my (hand) is clean!* Next, call some volunteers up to clean something. Repeat the same process, inviting the pupils to clean the item(s). You may also choose to have a pupil interact with Greenman and say your line *Let's clean it!*

Value activity: Being careful

Pretend to walk on a tightrope, wobbling from side to side. Have Greenman say *Be careful!* Reply *OK, Greenman.* Pretend to pick up something very heavy. Have Greenman say *Be careful!* Say *OK, Greenman.* Point out parts of the story when this value appears, for example, say *Be careful, Sam!*

Ask pupils in L1 why they think Greenman says *Be careful!* (because he doesn't want the children to get hurt). Pupils can tell you about times when someone said *Be careful!* to them.

Emotions: Being hurt

Look again at the places in the story where Sam and Nico are hurt. In L1, ask pupils about times when they hurt themselves. Talk about what part of the body they hurt, how they felt and what made them feel better.

Teacher Resources Worksheet 12: Look and circle.

Pass out the worksheet, or ask your helper. Say *Look at the girl, her finger hurts.* Point to the girl and her finger in the picture. Say *What does she need?* Point to the picture of the hand offering a ball. Say *Does she need a ball? No. Does she need a plaster? Yes! Circle the hand with a plaster.* Model how to do this on your own paper. Repeat the process with the next picture.

✏️ Activity Book page 18 – Investigate

Review the parts of the body vocabulary and the names of any animals pupils know.

Use a torch to introduce the idea of shadows. Then make different shapes with your hands, and help pupils notice the different shapes of the shadows. Make some different animal shadows for them to guess.

Direct pupils' attention to the pictures in the book and elicit the different animals they can see in the shadows (bird and rabbit). Then they find four more differences and circle all the differences with a pencil.

🙂 **Now you!** Ask different pupils to make shadow pictures for the rest of the class to guess. Pupils can also make shadow art by drawing around shadows. They could go outside on a sunny day and draw around each other's shadows at different times of day, noticing how the size of the shadows changes.

🙆 **I can do it.** Say *Well done!* after pupils make their shadow pictures. Pupils repeat the affirmation *I can do it* with you.

🌱 Help pupils understand the importance of sunlight for plants to grow. They can plant their own plants in areas of the school garden where it's the sunniest, or on a sunny windowsill.

Lesson 4

Lesson objective
To use TPR to review unit vocabulary through an action song.

Language
New: *round; Put your (hand) in/out. Shake it. Move your hand up. Turn around. the body*
Review: *up/down; colours*
Receptive: *Let's make a (circle). What comes next? Draw the (hand).*

Materials
Presentation Plus, PB page 41, Flashcards Unit 3, Class Audio, crayons, pencils. Optional: PB page 42, plasticine, AB page 19

 Use Presentation Plus to watch the action song video and the Forest Fun Activity Book yoga video. ▷

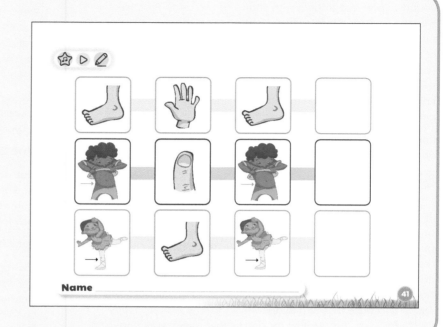

Name _____ 41

🍃 Starting the lesson

Settle the class with an opening routine (see Teacher's Book pages 8 and 9).

🍃 Active time

Warmer

Use the Unit 3 Flashcards to review the vocabulary.

Game: *Move your body*

This game will help prepare pupils for the Unit 3 action song. The main concepts are 'in', 'out' and the parts of the body. If the pupils are not already in a circle, say *Let's make a circle.* Have pupils hold hands to spread out and form a circle.

Stand in the inside of the circle and say *This is 'in'.* Go outside the circle and say *This is 'out'.* Say *Show me your hand.* Show the pupils how you put your hand up. Say *Now put your hand 'in'.* Model putting your hand inside the circle. Say *Put your hand 'out'.* Model holding your hand outside the circle. Repeat with different parts of the body.

In and out action song: Watch the video. Sing and do the actions.

 You may prefer to use the action song video to teach the pupils the actions and the song.

First, play the audio and hold up flashcards for the vocabulary words in the song. Invite the pupils to say the word when you hold up the card. The second time you play the song, do the actions to show the class. Next, have the pupils stand up *(Stand up, stand up, 1-2-3. Stand up, stand up tall with me).* Teach them the actions one by one as you say each line of the song.

Practise the actions for the song three or four times slowly, going through the song line by line. Then, play the audio track and do the actions together. Repeat until all of the class is participating in each action and singing some of the words.

🎧 30 In and out 🎵

*You put your **hand** in.*
(Move the hand to the centre of the circle.)

*You put your **hand** out.*
(Move the hand outside of the circle.)

Round and round.
(Move the hand in a circular motion.)

Shake it all about! (Shake the hand.)

*Move your **hand** up and turn around.* (Move the hand up and turn your whole body round.)

In, out, in, out. Stop! (Move the hand in and out of the centre quickly, stamp your foot.)

Repeat with: *leg, arm, finger, tummy, foot*

🍃 Table time

Say the Table time chant (see page 11).

Pupil's Book page 41. Worksheet 4: Draw what comes next.

Show pupils page 41 and walk around to check that everyone is on the correct page. Draw on the board a sequence of shapes: circle, square, circle, square, circle, and a blank space. Say the series aloud, then ask *What comes next?* Help the pupils to say *Square.* Draw a square in the blank space on the board. Direct the pupils' attention to page 41 and the first series of pictures. Say *Look: foot, hand, foot (pause) what comes next?* Elicit the answer *hand.* Say *Draw the hand.* Model in your own book or on the board. Repeat with the next two series of pictures (pupils draw a finger and a foot).

🍃 Goodbye

Follow the description on page 9.

🍃 Extra activities

📖 Pupil's Book page 42. Extra activity: Draw your favourite action in the song.

Sing the *In and out* action song (Track 30) again and ask the pupils which action they like. Do the action and say *I like to shake my leg.* Show a 'thumbs up' and smile. Ask *What do you like, (Mario)?* Help the pupil to say an action. Ask several pupils.

Show a prepared drawing of the action 'shake your leg'. Say again *I like to shake my leg.* Shrug your shoulders and point to the pupils as you say *What do you like? Draw.* Model drawing a picture.

Have pupils open their Pupil's Books to page 42 and make sure everyone is on the correct page. Walk around the class to be sure each pupil has understood. When they have finished, you may choose to have the children share their pictures with the class.

Make a plasticine body.

Before passing out plasticine, make an example in front of the class. Show pupils how you can make a body by pinching and pulling the plasticine and not necessarily breaking it up into pieces. Say *Look. What is it?* Begin to form a body from the plasticine. When you are finished, say *Where's the (leg)?* Have volunteers come up to point to the correct part.

Prepare to pass out a ball of plasticine to each pupil and say *One, two, three hands on your knees.* Show the class how they should keep their hands on their knees until they have permission to begin. When everyone has plasticine, look around and say *Look. Ready? Go.* Say this in a calm voice so that pupils know there is no need to rush. Observe the pupils as they work and help those who are struggling. Ask questions about different parts of the body as you walk around, engaging individual children.

When the pupils have completed their plasticine models, call out the parts of the body and have them point to them on their models. At the end of the activity, collect all of the figures and congratulate each pupil on their model.

✏️ Activity Book page 19 – Feel

Look at the activity in the book. Teach the word *tree* and explain that the children are doing the tree yoga pose. Pupils then do the activity – tracing around the tree and drawing themselves doing the pose.

☺ ▷ **Now you!** Pupils stand up and do some stretching exercises with you. You can also do some simple yoga poses with them – reviewing ones pupils learned in the Starter Level, as well as the bee pose from Unit 1. Demonstrate the tree yoga pose and ask pupils to copy you. Ask pupils to think of calming thoughts as they do the pose, e.g. birds singing in their tree, butterflies fluttering around. Pupils can watch the video for more practice. You may wish to review numbers *1–4* and pre-teach numbers *5* and *6* before you watch.

🧘 **I feel good.** Say *Oh, it's good to be a tree. I feel good. I feel calm.* Ask pupils in L1 if they feel calm, too, and encourage them to say *Yes.* Pupils repeat the affirmation *I feel good* with you.

🌱 Help pupils learn about the importance of trees and looking after them. Explain that trees provide a home for lots of animals.

Lesson 5

Lesson objective
To work on pre-writing skills and practise numbers through a song.

Language
New: number 5; the body
Review: shapes; colours; numbers 1–4; animals
Receptive: *How many (legs)? Let's draw a line. Let's trace the numbers.*

Materials
Presentation Plus, PB page 43, Flashcards Unit 3, Class Audio, crayons, pencils. Optional: PB page 44, groups of 5 classroom objects (books, pencils, crayons), homemade number cards 1–5, Teacher Resources Worksheet 13, AB page 20

 Use Presentation Plus to do the activities.

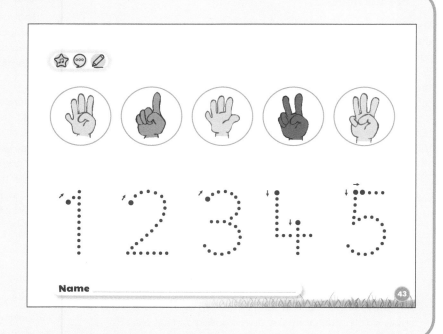

Name _____

🖐 Starting the lesson

Settle the class with an opening routine (see Teacher's Book pages 8 and 9).

🖐 Active time

Warmer

Review shapes, colours and numbers 1–4 (you can use the Routine Boards and the Flashcards on Presentation Plus).

Review parts of the body and numbers by counting how many of each part you have. Then call up two pupils and count how many of the parts of the body there are in total. Point to your own legs and say *There are two legs. One, two. (Lucía), come here please. How many legs? One, two, three, four.* Repeat with other parts of the body (arms, hands, tummy, feet, but not fingers).

Count to five.

Look at your hands, legs and arms and say *Where are there five?* Count your arms, legs, hands, tummy, feet again and finally say *My fingers! Look, one, two, three, four, five!* Point to different pupils and have them count their own fingers (only on one hand). Give several (or all) of the pupils a chance to participate individually.

Five fingers number song 1–5: Sing and count.

Pupils will continue to practise counting on their fingers with a new song. Play the song once, holding up your fingers for each number. When the song says 'and 5', act surprised and then confident (nod your head as if you feel proud).

Say the song without the audio track, pausing after each line to look at the pupils and be sure they are following along and moving

their fingers. Practise this way twice, then play the song again for pupils to join in with the words and actions. Continue repeating the song until all of the pupils are singing most of the words and all of the numbers.

 Five fingers

1, 2, 3, 4 and 5!
Count with me, count to 5!

Move 1 finger: 1, 1!
Move 2 fingers: 2, 2!
Move 3 fingers: 3, 3!
Move 4 fingers: 4, 4!
Move 5 fingers: 5, 5!

1, 2, 3, 4 and 5!

🖐 Table time

Say the Table time chant (see page 11).

 Pupil's Book page 43. Worksheet 5: Count, match and trace.

Show pupils page 43 and walk around to check that everyone is on the correct page. Point to the first hand and say *Let's count the fingers, one, two, three, four!* Point to number 4. Yes, now let's draw a line. Show how to draw a line from the four fingers to the number 4. Do the same with the other pictures/numbers, or, if you think pupils can complete the activity independently, gesture drawing lines and say *Draw the lines.* Then point to the numbers and say *1, 2, 3, 4, 5. Let's trace the numbers.* Show how to follow the arrows to do this. Give the pupils time to trace the five numbers while you walk around and monitor.

🍃 Goodbye

Follow the description on page 9.

🍃 Extra activities

📑 Pupil's Book page 44. Extra activity: Draw and colour five animals.

Say *Look at the animals.* Elicit or review the names of the animals, which pupils learnt in Starter Level *(dog, bird, cat, fish* and *turtle).* Say *Let's draw.* Draw each of the animals on the board and then count them *One, two three, four, five.* Have pupils draw and count the animals (one animal in each space of the frame). Monitor as pupils complete the activity. If they prefer, pupils could also draw five of one animal, e.g. five fish.

Game: *Find the number*

Prepare different classroom objects (pencils, crayons, books, etc.), making sure you have at least five of each. Place the objects in the centre of the circle. To play the game, follow the description on page 18.

Listen and chant.

Say the following lines while pointing to each item on your own body. Say the lines as a military-style chant and act like a soldier (a bit stiff and formal). Have the pupils repeat after you: *One nose, two legs, one tummy, two feet, two arms, two hands, five fingers.*

Teacher Resources Worksheet 13: Trace your hand.

Pass out the worksheet or ask your helper. Hold up a sample worksheet and show how to hold your hand to the paper and trace with the opposite hand (you may want to do this on the board). Be sure to show that the pencil (or marker) is very close to your hand while you trace. Monitor and offer help as pupils trace their own hands. You may wish to have them count their fingers and decorate their hand print when they have finished tracing.

📝 Activity Book page 20 – Practise

Review colours and numbers with the class.

Demonstrate the activity: choose five coloured crayons. Point to the paint blobs on the page, and say *Hmm, I think 1 is … (red)!* Colour the blob. Repeat with the other blobs. Pupils choose five colours and colour in the key. Make it clear that they do not have to choose the same colours as you.

Model how to colour in the main picture to match the key.

Pupils compare their pictures to see the different effects that different colours have produced.

🙆 **I try hard.** Pupils look at their pictures. In L1, ask if the activity was easy or difficult. Praise them for their efforts. Pupils repeat the affirmation *I try hard* with you.

☺ **Now you!** Pupils can go outside and try to find five insects or spiders. Make sure they understand that they can look at these creatures, but shouldn't touch them or pick them up as they might hurt them.

🌱 Help pupils understand they must not touch and break a spider's web. Explain that a web is a spider's home.

Lesson 6

Lesson objective
To consolidate all unit content.

Language
Review: the body; Big Book language structures
Receptive: *Don't look. What's your card? Find and stick.*

Materials
Presentation Plus, Greenman Puppet, Big Book story Unit 3, PB page 45, Flashcards Units 1, 2 and 3, Class Audio, Stickers Unit 3, 2 clothes pegs, crayons, pencils. Optional: AB page 21

 Use Presentation Plus to play the games. ✛☆

🍃 Starting the lesson

Settle the class with an opening routine (see Teacher's Book pages 8 and 9).

🍃 Active time

Warmer

Review Flashcards from Units 1, 2, and 3 by holding each one up and saying the vocabulary word with the pupils. Say *What's this? Is it a (slide)?* (wait for pupils to respond) *Oh! It's a leg!* Exchange different vocabulary words and then confirm the correct answer. You may wish to use the audio of the Unit 3 vocabulary to review (Track 27).

Game: *What's my card?*

Bring two volunteers to the centre of the circle. Use a clothes peg to attach a flashcard to one pupil's back, make sure he/she doesn't turn around or look at the flashcard. Do the same with a different flashcard on the back of the other volunteer. Say *Don't look!* Show each volunteer the other one's back so they know what the flashcard is. Make sure that they each know the word, if not whisper it to them. Say *Now, (Lucía), what's your card?* Say *Is it a (hand)?* Point to your hand. Have the pupil repeat the question. Help the other pupil to answer *yes* or *no.* Have the pupils take turns asking questions until they guess their own flashcard. Repeat several times with different volunteers.

🍃 Story review

Say the Story time chant *It's story time, story time, open the Big Book and look inside* and motion opening a book. Reread the story, inviting the pupils to participate in saying the words or lines that they know.

▷ Alternatively, you may want to play the story video.

🍃 Table time

Say the Table time chant (see page 11).

📖 Pupil's Book page 45. Worksheet 6: Find, stick and say.

Help the pupils to find page 45 in the Pupil's Book and locate the stickers for Unit 3. Say *Find and stick the picture.* Have Greenman repeat each word several times as pupils look for the correct sticker to put in each place. Monitor the children as they work and encourage them along, or give gesture clues. Repeat with each vocabulary word. When they have finished, have pupils point to each sticker and say the word.

🍃 Goodbye

Follow the description on page 9.

📝 Activity Book page 21 – Care

Review some of the emotions pupils know (including *happy, sad, excited, worried* and *hurt*). Pupils look at the page and decide if the insect is happy/excited or sad/hurt. Explain that he needs a place to rest, and introduce the idea of the insect hotel. You could bring an insect hotel to class to show pupils, or use photos.

Show pupils how to help the insect find the hotel by tracing the path through the maze. Pupils trace the path, first with their fingers, then with their pencils.

🙌 **I care for animals.** Praise pupils for helping the insect find shelter. Pupils can also think about other ways they can care for insects, pets or wild animals. Pupils repeat the affirmation *I care for animals* with you.

☺ **Now you!** Pupils can make an insect hotel from sticks, leaves, toilet rolls, bark, etc in an old plastic bottle. They can look at it every day and notice what insects are using it.

🌱 Help pupils understand why animals need a habitat, and what we can do to protect their natural habitats.

To end the unit, pupils circle the squirrel on page 2.

Extra Phonics Lesson

Lesson objective
To introduce a new phonics sound ('l').

Language
New: *leg, long*

Materials
Presentation Plus, Greenman Puppet, PB page 46, downloadable Phonics Flashcards, Class Audio, crayons, pencils. Optional: Teacher Resources Worksheet 14

🐛 Phonics time

Warmer

Show pupils the *l* Phonics Flashcard. Read the word, then segment the sound. Say *Look at the picture: There is a leg. Listen to the sound: l. Listen and repeat: l-l-l leg.* Point to the Phonics Flashcard and say the sound and word three times, asking different pupils to repeat after you.

📖 Pupil's Book page 46. 1. Listen and say the *l* letter sound.

Have pupils open their books to page 46. Say *Point to the leg* and model pointing to the leg in activity 1. Have Greenman say *l-l-leg, l-l-long, l-l-look, l-l-leg, l-l-long,* stretching out the 'l' sound as much as possible. Play the audio and have pupils listen and repeat the sound and word. Play the track three times.

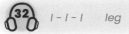

32 *l – l – l   leg*

📖 Pupil's Book page 46. 2. Sing the song.

Show pupils the picture in activity 2. Play the song. Point to items in the picture to help pupils understand meaning. After playing the track three times, say it slowly, and have pupils repeat each line, while looking at the picture. Continue repeating until pupils are saying at least the *long, long legs* part of the song.

33
L, Long, long legs!
Look at my long, long legs.
I can play on the flowers,
Yes, I can play on the flowers,
With my long, long legs!

📖 Pupil's Book page 46. 3. How many legs? Listen and circle the number.

Show pupils activity 3 in your book. Elicit the names for each of the pictures (*table, girl, dog* and *chair*). Say *Now listen. How many legs?* Play the audio, pause after the first sentence and say *Table. How many legs?* Elicit the answer *One.* Say *Yes, one leg. Let's circle.* Model circling the number *1* in your book. Play the rest of the audio, pausing after each section to say *Circle the number.* Review the activity as a class.

34
A table. One leg.
A girl. Two legs.
A dog. Four legs.
A chair. Three legs.

🐛 Extra activities

Teacher Resources Worksheet 14: Trace the spider's legs. Trace and colour the flower.

Prepare one worksheet for each pupil in advance. Say the *l* letter sound and the word *legs.* Then point to the spider's legs on the worksheet and say *Trace the spider's legs.* Model how to trace using an example worksheet. Next say the word *legs,* emphasising the *l* sound and have the pupils repeat. Do the same for the flower, then have the pupils colour the flower.

Unit 4: It's too small!

Lesson 1

Lesson objective
To introduce the main vocabulary for the unit (clothing).

Language
New: *boots, coat, dress, hat, jumper, trousers; pink, purple*
Review: weather; colours
Receptive: *What is it? Pass the cards. Stop! Let's colour it (purple).*

Materials
Presentation Plus, pictures of a sunny/cloudy/windy/rainy/snowy day, Greenman Puppet, Big Book story Unit 4, PB page 47, Flashcards Unit 4, Class Audio, crayons, pencils. Optional: PB page 48, pink and purple objects, AB page 22

 Use Presentation Plus to watch the unit introduction video and vocabulary song video. ▷

4 It's too small!

Name
47

Starting the lesson

Settle the class with an opening routine (see Teacher's Book pages 8 and 9).

Active time

Welcome to Unit 4

▷ Tell pupils that you are about to start a new unit. Play the Unit 4 introduction video to introduce the unit topic. Pause the video at different points and ask, in L1, what the children can see and what they think they will learn about in this unit.

Warmer

Review weather vocabulary (you could use the Routine Boards on Presentation Plus). Have pupils show *hot* by stretching their arms out and *cold* by shivering. Show pupils an image of the weather and ask if it is *hot* or *cold* in the picture. Help them to act out their answer. Say *It's sunny. Hot or cold?* Elicit the response *Hot.*

Game: *Pass, stop and say*

Have Greenman take out the Unit 4 Flashcards. Say *What's this Greenman, new words?* Act very excited about the new words. Take each flashcard out individually and say *Look! A hat! Repeat, class, a hat! What is it? (A hat.)* While you say the word, use gestures to reinforce the concept (act out putting on an imaginary hat). Repeat this process with each card.

Have the children stand up. Say the Stand up transition chant *Stand up, stand up, 1-2-3. Stand up, stand up tall with me!* Show

each flashcard again. This time have the pupils do the action for each article of clothing. Repeat the process with each card. See page 18 for a description of how to play this game.

At this point, your may wish to use the audio of the unit vocabulary to listen and repeat as a class.

 boots, coat, dress, hat, jumper, trousers

I'm cold song: Sing and do the actions.

While pupils remain standing, play the *I'm cold* song for the class. Hold up the corresponding flashcard when that word is mentioned in the song. Encourage pupils to use their actions to show the words. Next, say the song line by line, slowly, enunciating the words and doing the actions. Then, repeat the song three times with the audio track or until most pupils are participating by doing the actions and singing some of the words.

 I'm cold

I'm cold, I'm cold. (Wrap your arms around yourself shivering.)

It's very, very, cold. (Continue shivering.)

Where's your jumper? (Look around with a questioning gesture.)

Put it on! (Pretend to put on a jumper.)

Repeat with: *Where's your hat? Put it on! Where are your trousers/boots? Put them on. Where's your dress/coat? Put it on!*

▷ You may wish to watch the vocabulary song video at this point.

🍃 Story time

Say the Story time chant *It's story time, story time, open the Big Book and look inside* and motion opening a book. Open the Big Book to the first two pages of the Unit 4 story. Say *What do we see? Oh, look! Rabbit's got a jumper! Is it hot? Is it cold?*

After identifying all of the vocabulary words, close the book.

🍃 Table time

Say the Table time chant (see page 11).

📑 Pupil's Book page 47. Worksheet 1: Look, colour and say.

Show pupils page 47 and walk around to check that everyone is on the correct page. Point to each item of clothing and elicit the name. Then ask about the colours of the clothes. Review *red*, *blue* and *green* and present the new colours: *pink* and *purple*. Say *Let's colour! Let's colour the coat. Let's colour it purple!* Hold up the flashcard for *coat* and a purple crayon. Model colouring the coat in your book. Repeat with each picture, not necessarily in order. Monitor pupils' work by walking around the room and helping those in need.

When all of the pictures have been coloured, point to each item and say the colour and vocabulary word for pupils to repeat *Purple coat, repeat, purple coat.*

🍃 Goodbye

Follow the description on page 9.

🍃 Extra activities

📑 Pupil's Book page 48. Extra activity: Draw and colour you with your favourite winter clothes.

Say *In winter I like my coat. My coat is purple.* Model drawing a purple coat on the figure in your book on page 48. Ask a pupil *Do you like your hat? What colour is it? Wow – it's a yellow hat!* Mime putting on a hat and use a yellow crayon to show *yellow*. Place the flashcards on the board or another place in the class where everyone can see them. Direct the pupils' attention to page 48. Point to the flashcards and to the figure in the book. Say *Draw and colour winter clothes you like!* Monitor pupils to check for understanding.

Game: *Touch the colour*

Set out purple and pink objects. Follow the description on page 19.

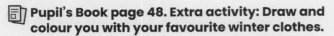 Activity Book page 22 – Observe

Review colours and clothes. Introduce the topic of colours in nature, by pointing to different objects you have brought to class, or to different items in photos, and asking what colour they are.

Look at the book. Show pupils the individual pictures in the key and elicit/say the names of the different natural materials, in English and L1. Elicit the different colours the natural materials might be. Encourage pupils to think of more unusual ones, e.g. blue and red for the feathers as well as brown, black and white. You may also wish to talk about the colours leaves can be in different seasons and the different colours flowers can be.

Pupils then choose a colour for each of the materials in the key and colour them in. Encourage them to choose colours that naturally occur in nature, and teach additional colours, as appropriate. Pupils can also choose colours suitable for a particular season, for example autumnal shades of orange, yellow, red and brown for the leaves and bracken.

Show pupils how to find and colour the materials in the collage in the same colours as they have chosen for the key.

👁️ **I look carefully.** Look at the stick people pictures and say *What beautiful colours. Well done!* Remind pupils how important it is to take time to look around carefully and learn from their surroundings. Pupils repeat the affirmation *I look carefully* with you.

☺ **Now you!** Pupils can go on a colour safari after school with their parents as a home-school connection activity. Encourage them to look for all the different colours in nature and to talk about the colours of the things they saw, when they are back in class. Alternatively, go for a walk around the school grounds and have pupils observe and talk about the different colours they see.

🌱 Help pupils appreciate colours in nature and also the changing of the seasons. Pupils can find out which trees lose their leaves in the autumn and why, and which trees have the brightest autumn leaf colours.

Lesson 2

Lesson objective
To present the key structures for the unit.

Language
New: *Your/The (dress) is/are too (small). Put on your (boots). Take off your (jumper). pink, purple;* clothes
Review: *good/naughty, clean/dirty;* weather; colours; numbers 1–5
Receptive: *I say, you do. You can't wear your (dress). Point to the (dress). Is it different? Let's circle.*

Materials
Presentation Plus, Greenman Puppet, Big Book story Unit 4, PB page 49, Flashcards Unit 4, Class Audio, sticky tape/tack, crayons, pencils. Optional: PB page 50, Teacher Resources Worksheet 15, AB page 23

 Use Presentation Plus to watch the story video. ▷

Name _____ 49

🍃 Starting the lesson

Settle the class with an opening routine (see Teacher's Book pages 8 and 9).

🍃 Active time

Warmer

Place the Unit 4 Flashcards on different walls around the classroom, in advance. Have Greenman ask *Where's the (coat)?* Greenman looks around the room for the flashcard of the coat. Point it out to the pupils. Repeat this process with the other five vocabulary words.

Listen and do.

Say the Stand up chant (see page 10). You will say different actions from Units 1–4 for the pupils to act out. Say *Time to act! I say, you do!* Say the series of actions, pausing after each one to do an action for the pupils to copy. Say *You are cold! Brrrr! You are good! Smile! You go up!* (stand on tiptoes) *You go down!* (crouch down) *Your (face) is dirty! Clean your (face)! You are clean! Hooray!* Then say the sentences again for children to do the actions.

Game: *Say it! Mime it!*

Call on a volunteer. He/She will select a flashcard. Say *What is it?* Help the pupil to say the word. Whisper the sentence to the pupil for him/her to repeat to the class, *Put on your (jumper).* Act out what the pupil has said and encourage the class to do the same. Repeat with different cards and different pupils. Then play the game again with *Take off your (boots).*

🍃 Story time

Say the Story time chant *It's story time, story time, open the Big Book and look inside* and motion opening a book. Elicit vocabulary learned in the previous lesson on the first page of the story. Greenman can ask *What is this?* while you give examples of answers for the pupils to repeat. Identify the characters: Nico, Sam, Greenman and Rabbit. Say *Is it hot? Is it cold?* Have the pupils do actions to show *cold*.

Read the story or play the audio version (Track 37), pausing to use facial and hand gestures to help convey meaning.

 Alternatively, you may want to play the story video.

🎧37 It's too small!

It's winter time. It's windy. Sam and Nico are cold. Rabbit is sad.
'Hello, Rabbit. What's the matter?' says Greenman.
'Hello, Greenman. I'm hungry!' says Rabbit.
'Where are your carrots?'
'I haven't got any carrots. Look, the birds are eating them!'
'Oh, no!' says Greenman.
'Oh, no! My hat! I'm cold!' says Sam.
'I'm cold. Let's go home!' says Nico.
'Let's put on winter clothes!' says Sam.
'Good idea!' says Nico.

Sam is at home. She's putting on her
winter clothes.
'Sam, you can't wear your pink dress,' says Mum.
'You can't wear your purple boots.'
'I like my pink dress!' says Sam.
'I like my purple boots!'
*'Your dress is too small. Your boots are too small.
Please, take them off!'*

Nico is at home. He's putting on his winter clothes.
'Nico, you can't wear your winter jumper,'
says Dad. *'You can't wear your winter trousers!'*
'I like my winter jumper!' says Nico.
'I like my winter trousers!'
*'Your jumper is too small. Your trousers
are too small. Please, take them off!'*

'You can't put the clothes in the bin!' says Sam.
*'But I can't wear the jumper. I can't wear the
trousers!'* says Nico.
'What can we do with them?'
'Greenman!' say Sam and Nico.

'Look!' says Nico. *'Greenman is wearing your
purple boots, my winter jumper and my
winter trousers!'*
'He's a scarecrow. The birds are scared!' says Sam.
'Rabbit has got carrots to eat.'
'And we are recycling the clothes!'
'Boo!' says Greenman.

🍃 Table time

Say the Table time chant (see page 11).

📑 Pupil's Book page 49. Worksheet 2: Find and circle the five differences.

Show pupils page 49 and walk around to check that everyone is on the correct page. Point to the first picture, say *Sam's dress is pink. Point to the dress. The boots are too small. Point to the boots. The hat is too big. Point to the hat. Mum's dress is blue. Point to the dress. The boots are black. Point to the boots.* Walk around the classroom as you call out and point in your book. Pause after each item and check if pupils are pointing to the correct things.

Point to the second picture, say *What's different? Let's look. Sam's dress is red. Hmmm. Is it different?* Point back and forth between the two pictures to show that you want the pupils to compare. *The dress is different. It's red not pink. Let's circle.* Model how to circle Sam's dress. Repeat the process with the other items, or, if you think pupils can finish the activity independently, say *Find the differences.* Then review the activity together. Say *What's different?* The pupils may say *boots* and point to Sam's boots. Point between the pictures again and say *Yes, the boots are too small. The boots are too big.* Encourage pupils to repeat each sentence. Repeat with Sam's hat, Mum's dress, and Mum's boots: *The dress/boots is/ are (blue).*

🍃 Goodbye

Follow the description on page 9.

Follow the description on page 9.

🍃 Extra activities

Pupil's Book page 50. Extra activity: Draw and colour clothes on the scarecrow.

Direct pupils' attention to page 50 and check that they are on the correct page. Say *What's this? No clothes! Let's put clothes on the scarecrow. A jumper? Yes? OK, let's draw a jumper.* Show pupils how to draw a jumper on the scarecrow. Continue with other clothing items.

Teacher Resources Worksheet 15: Trace the pictures.

Pass out the worksheet, or ask your helper. Hold up a sample worksheet to show the children. Say *Look, it's Sam with a hat, dress, coat and boots! Let's trace Sam's clothes!* Show how to trace the unfinished side to complete the picture of Sam. Repeat this process with the picture of Nico.

Say *Put on/Take off your (hat)* and have pupils mime the actions.

📖 Activity Book page 23 – Find and make

Pupils find natural materials and use them to make and decorate a nature hat. Pupils can find the natural materials outside, either before or during the lesson, or alternatively bring the materials to class for pupils to find. As well as the natural materials (bendy twigs, feathers, bracken, flowers and grasses), you will also need to provide string or twine.

Review the word *hat.* Show pupils the individual pictures in the book and talk about the different natural materials in English and L1. Draw their attention to the picture of the nature hat and tell pupils they are going to make one, and decorate it with the natural materials. Encourage pupils to look and talk about how the natural materials are used to make the hat.

Pupils look for the natural materials, either outside or among the materials that have been brought to the classroom. When they find one of the items in the pictures, they circle it.

🙂 **Now you!** Pupils make their hats with the materials they find. Help pupils make the base for the hat first, by twisting the twigs and tying them into place with string. Alternatively, you could do this before class. Pupils then decorate their hats with the natural materials.

🙌 **I can do it.** Compare pupils' hats and say *These are well made. Well done!* Remind pupils of how many things they can do. Pupils repeat the affirmation *I can do it* with you.

🌱 Explain to pupils that they should only use flowers that are very plentiful in their hats – for example daisies, buttercups, dandelions, or flowers that have fallen to the ground.

Lesson ③

Lesson objective
To introduce a contrasting concept (big/small), and a value (recycling).

Language
New: *The (boots) is/are too (small).* clothes
Review: *big/small; weather; shapes; colours*
Receptive: *Let's make a (small circle). Draw a (triangle). Show me. What comes next? Let's circle.*

Materials
Presentation Plus, Greenman Puppet, Big Book story Unit 4, PB page 51, Pop-outs Unit 4, glue sticks, Class Audio, crayons, pencils. Optional: PB page 52, plasticine, recyclable objects (lids, plastic bottles, etc.), Teacher Resources Worksheet 16, scissors, AB page 24

 Use Presentation Plus to do the activity.

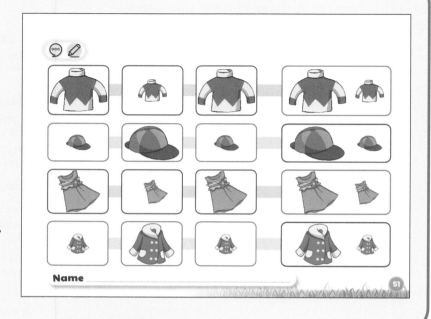

Name _____

🍃 Starting the lesson

Settle the class with an opening routine (see Teacher's Book pages 8 and 9).

🍃 Active time

Warmer

Review the words for shapes (you can use the Routine Boards on Presentation Plus).

Make big and small shapes.

In this activity, the children will either make a shape with their body on their own, or join other pupils to make a very big shape.

Do the Stand up chant (see page 10). Help the pupils spread out so that they have space to each make a shape with their own body. Choose a volunteer, or your helper to help demonstrate. Say *(Mario), can you make a small circle with your body?* Have Greenman try to curl his body into a circle. Say *Can you do it?* You may want to do the example yourself. When the pupil has made a circle, say *Well done, everyone, let's make a small circle!* Help the pupils to do this. Say *Very good, a small circle. Let's make a big circle! Everyone together.* Walk around and help the pupils to form the shape, either sitting down or laying on their sides. Say *Is it a small circle? No! Is it a big circle? Yes! Very good, let's make a small triangle.* Repeat the process with different shapes.

Game: *Air drawings*

Follow the description on page 18.

🍃 Story time

Say the Story time chant *It's story time, story time, open the Big Book and look inside* and motion opening a book. Take out the Big Book and review the unit vocabulary. Ask: *Where's the dress? What's this? What colour is it?*

You may call on individual pupils to come up and point things out in the book. Allow pupils to point rather than say the word if they are shy.

Then, point out the parts of the story where we can see small items – the dress, boots, jumper and trousers are all too small.

Reread the story or listen to the Class Audio (Track 37).

▷ You may also choose to use the story video, pausing the video rather than pointing to pictures.

🍃 Table time

Say the Table time chant (see page 11).

Do the pop-out activity.

Direct pupils' attention to the sample pop-out that you have prepared: Greenman with different items of clothing to attach. Hold up the different clothing items and say *Let's put on the boots. They're perfect! Let's put on something different. Let's put on the hat. Yes! Very good!* The pupils should be joining in. Say *This is perfect. Very good. Now you can do it!*

Show pupils how to take out the pop-out pieces carefully. Monitor as they do this and help as needed.

When all the pupils have finished, say *Show me Greenman.* Hold up the pop-out. Say *Greenman is feeling cold. Show me the trousers. Put on the trousers.* Model how to stick the trousers on Greenman. Repeat with the other items of clothing until everyone has 'dressed' Greenman. Monitor and help pupils as necessary. Remind pupils how to put away their pop-outs.

📖 Pupil's Book page 51 Worksheet 3: Say *big* or *small*. Then circle what comes next.

Show pupils page 51 in the Pupil's Book and walk around to check that everyone is on the correct page.

Draw a series of shapes on the board: circle, square, circle, and then a circle above a square. Say *What comes next?* Elicit the response *Square*. Repeat with big circles and small circles. Now, point to page 51 in your book. Point to the first row and start the pupils off with the words, later pausing to give them time to say what is in the picture on their own if they can. *Big jumper, small jumper, big jumper, what comes next?* Elicit the response *Small jumper!* Say *Well done, let's circle the small jumper.* Repeat until pupils are ready to continue the activity on their own. Monitor their work and help pupils who are having difficulties.

Review the answers by having pupils repeat the patterns.

🍃 Goodbye

Follow the description on page 9.

🍃 Extra activities

📖 Pupil's Book page 52. Extra activity: Draw something big and something small.

Show the pupils a big and small version of an object that you have in the classroom. Say *I've got a big (book). I've got a small (book).* Repeat with other big and small items or draw pictures on the board. Say *Let's draw something big and something small.* Model in your own book and monitor as pupils complete the activity.

Make big and small plasticine shapes.

The pupils will use plasticine to make a big or small shape. Before passing out plasticine to the class, model an example. Make a small triangle and say *Small triangle. Repeat, small triangle.* Do the same with a big triangle.

Prepare to pass out a ball of plasticine to each child and say *One, two, three, hands on your knees.* Model to show that pupils should keep their hands on their knees until they have permission to begin. When everyone has plasticine, look around and say *Look. Ready? Go. Big circle.* Say this in a calm voice so that pupils know there is no need to rush. Monitor the pupils as they work and help those who struggle. When pupils have had time to finish the shape, say *One, two, three (big circle)!* Everyone holds up their shape. Congratulate the class. Repeat with *triangle* and *square*, varying the size.

Emotions: Feeling cold

Look at the part of the story where Sam and Nico are feeling cold. In L1, talk about times pupils feel cold and what they can do, e.g. wrap a towel around themselves after getting out of a swimming pool.

Value activity: Recycling

Point out the Big Book page where the children are talking about throwing clothing in the bin. Say *The children can recycle! They can share!* Take out the recycled objects that you have brought to class. Hold up each object and say *Can I recycle it?* The children say *Yes!* You could also make a 'Recycling station' where pupils can bring in items from home that can be recycled as classroom manipulatives, like lids and bottle caps.

Teacher Resources Worksheet 16: Cut and stick.

Pass out the worksheet or ask your helper. Point to the dress meant for Sam that is too small. Say *Look, a dress for Sam. No ... it's too small! Let's put it in the recycling bin.* Have pupils cut it out and glue it on/next to the recycling bin. *And this* (point to the one that fits) *Too big? No ... it fits!* Have pupils cut it out and glue it on Sam. Repeat the same process for Nico's trousers, recycling the trousers that are too big.

✏️ Activity Book page 24 – Investigate

Review *big, small, rainy* and the clothes you wear in rainy weather.

Show the picture in the book. Talk about the weather and the clothes the child is wearing. Use the picture to teach the word *puddle* and elicit which puddle is big and small. Have pupils trace around the outlines of the puddles.

Asks pupils to guess which puddle will make the biggest splash and why (big and deep puddles make a big splash). Show pupils how to match the puddles with the correct size of splash. They can also colour the picture in and draw themselves jumping in another puddle on the page.

😊 **Now you!** On a day when there has been a lot of rainfall, pupils can measure the size of puddles and test out the size of the splashes for themselves.

🙆 **I am interested in things.** In L1, discuss what pupils learned from their puddle jumping, and if they were right in guessing which puddles would make the biggest splash. Remind pupils that it's good to be interested in things, and that they learn by investigating and experimenting with what they find around them. Encourage pupils to repeat the affirmation *I am interested in things* with you.

🌱 Talk about how we can have fun in the rain and enjoy the sensory experience – the smell, feel and taste of rain as we play in it. Help pupils to also understand the importance of rain for the Earth.

Lesson 4

Lesson objective

To use TPR to review unit vocabulary through an action song.

Language

New: *pink, purple; Put on your (hat). Take off your (hat). clothes*
Review: weather; colours
Receptive: *Let's follow the paths.*

Materials

Presentation Plus, PB page 53, Flashcards Unit 4, Class Audio, crayons, pencils. Optional: PB page 54, small hoop, clothes (2 of each: hats, coats, boots, trousers dresses, jumpers), AB page 25

 Use Presentation Plus to watch the action song video. ▷

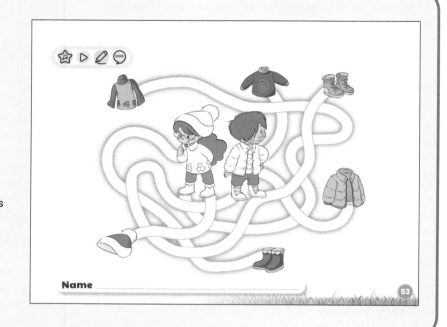

Name _____
53

🍂 Starting the lesson

Settle the class with an opening routine (see Teacher's Book pages 8 and 9).

🍂 Active time

Warmer

Play the game *Remember the cards*. Follow the description on page 19.

Game: *Follow the leader*

This game practises clothing vocabulary and actions. Have pupils follow you in a line doing the action that you say. Say *Let's jump.* Pupils continue jumping until you say *Stop! Now put on your (hat)!* Repeat *Put on your (hat)!* Continue with a different action, e.g. walking, jumping, swimming, etc, and say *Stop! Take off your (hat)!* Repeat with the different clothing items, modelling each action.

It's cold today action song: Watch the video. Sing and do the actions.

▷ You may prefer to use the action song video to teach the pupils the actions and the song.

First, play the audio and hold up flashcards for the vocabulary words in the song. Invite the pupils to say the word when you hold up the card. The second time you play the song, do the actions to show the class. Next, have the pupils stand up *(Stand up, stand up, 1-2-3. Stand up, stand up tall with me!).* Teach them the actions one by one as you say each line of the song.

Practise the actions for the song three or four times slowly, going through the song line by line. Then, play the audio track and do the actions together. Repeat until all of the class is participating in each action and singing some of the words.

38 🎧 It's cold today 🎵🎵

It's cold today, it's cold today.
(Bundle your arms around you and shiver.)

Put on your jumper and go out to play.
(Put on an imaginary jumper, run in place.)

Put on your jumper, it's cold today!
(Put on an imaginary jumper, shiver.)

It's cold today, it's cold today.
(Bundle your arms around you and shiver.)

Put on your trousers and go out to play.
(Put on imaginary trousers, run in place.)

Put on your jumper. (Put on an imaginary jumper.)

Put on your trousers, it's cold today!
(Put on imaginary trousers, bundle your arms around you and shiver.)

Add on: *boots, coat, hat*

🍂 Table time

Say the Table time chant (see page 11).

📖 Pupil's Book page 53. Worksheet 4: Follow the paths to find Sam and Nico's clothes. Then say.

Show pupils page 53 and walk around to check that everyone is on the correct page. Say *Oh no! Sam and Nico need to find their clothes! Let's follow the paths to help them!* Model in your own book tracing a line with your finger from Sam to Sam's boots. Have pupils copy you and then draw the line with a pencil. Say *Very good, now find more clothes for Sam.* Walk around the class and monitor as the pupils work. When they have finished, invite volunteers to hold up their books and follow the paths to Sam's clothes. Elicit the response from the class, e.g. *boots* or *red boots.* Repeat the same process with Nico's clothes, using a different coloured pencil.

🍃 Goodbye

Follow the description on page 9.

🍃 Extra activities

📖 Pupil's Book page 54. Extra activity: Trace and colour the clothes.

Pupils trace the lines for each item of clothing and then colour them in. Say *Where are the trousers? Where's the dress? Let's trace the lines with a pencil.* Give pupils time to do this, then say *Let's colour the dress and the trousers.* Monitor the pupils as they work asking questions to individual pupils such as *What colour are the trousers?* When pupils have finished, you may choose to have them share their pictures and say the colours they chose for the clothing.

Game: *The hoop game*

Follow the description on page 19.

Game: *Dress up*

Bring in some clothes for dress up. Put the clothing items in the middle of the circle. Have two volunteers go to the centre of the circle. Say different clothing items for the pupils to race to put on over their clothes, e.g. *Put on your (coat).* Help the pupils to choose the correct items. Repeat the same process with other pupils and clothing items.

✏️ Activity Book page 25 – Practise

Review the words for clothes.

Introduce the idea of doing a bark rubbing. If you have an outdoor classroom, you can demonstrate doing an actual bark rubbing on a tree. Alternatively, make a bark rubbing before the class and show this in class with a photo of the tree the pattern came from.

Pupils look at the clothes in the book. Point out that the patterns on the clothes come from bark rubbings. Encourage pupils to point to the clothes that have the same patterns.

Point to the first row and elicit each item of clothing as you point to it. When you get to the blank square, ask *What comes next?* Elicit the response *Trousers!* Say *Well done! Let's draw some trousers.* Monitor and help while pupils complete the rest of the sequencing activity. Give them time to compare their ideas in pairs.

🙌 **I try hard.** When pupils have finished the activity, congratulate them and encourage them to congratulate each other. Find out if they thought copying the clothes was easy or difficult. Encourage them to repeat the affirmation *I try hard* with you.

🙂 **Now you!** Pupils can make bark rubbings themselves or, alternatively, make rubbings from other surfaces around them; brick walls, tarmac in the playground, etc. They can then draw an item of clothing onto the patterned paper (as big as possible) and cut it out. You could make a classroom display with their patterned clothes.

🌱 Help pupils to understand that different trees have different bark. They can also learn how important bark is to the life of a tree, in a similar way as our skin is important to us. Explain that they mustn't pull bark off a tree or damage it.

Lesson 5

Lesson objective
To work on pre-writing skills and practise numbers through a song.

Language
New: *Put on your (trousers). clothes*
Review: colours; weather; numbers 1–5
Receptive: *Give me (three) blocks. Let's count the (boots). Draw a line. Let's trace the numbers.*

Materials
Presentation Plus, PB page 55, Flashcards Unit 4, Class Audio, coloured building blocks, pieces of paper numbered 1–5, crayons, pencils. Optional: PB page 56, 1 A4 piece of paper per pupil (divided into 4 sections numbered 1–4), Teacher Resources Worksheet 17, AB page 26

 Use Presentation Plus to do the activities.

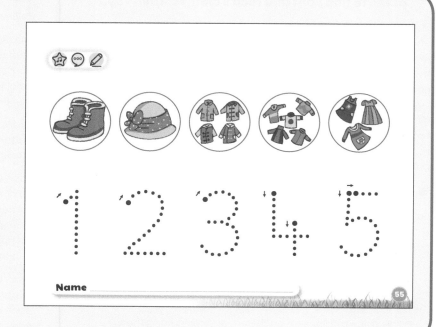

Name _____

🐌 Starting the lesson

Settle the class with an opening routine (see Teacher's Book pages 8 and 9).

🐌 Active time

Warmer

Place coloured building blocks in the centre of the circle. Practise counting them in groups of one to five. Then practise counting and grouping them by colour. *How many red blocks? One, two, three. Three red blocks! Repeat. Three red blocks.*

Game: *Find the number*

Pupils remain sitting in a circle with the blocks in the centre. Play this game by following the description on page 18 and using the coloured building blocks. Optional: expand with *(María), give me three (red) blocks.*

Clothes number song 1–5: Sing, count and do the actions.

Say *Let's practise numbers and clothes!* Play the song once, holding up your fingers for each number. Next, say the song, line by line, modelling the actions. Practise this way twice, then play the song again for pupils to join in with the words and actions. Continue repeating the song until all of the pupils are singing most of the words and all of the numbers.

---

39 **Clothes** 🎵

Number 1. (Hold up one finger.)

Put on your trousers. (Put on imaginary trousers.)

Number 2. (Hold up two fingers.)

Put on your jumper! (Put on an imaginary jumper.)

Number 3 (Hold up three fingers.)

Put on your boots! (Put on imaginary boots.)

Number 4. (Hold up four fingers.)

Put on your coat! (Put on an imaginary coat.)

Number 5. (Hold up five fingers.)

Put on your hat! (Put on an imaginary hat.)

Now you are ready, (Hold your hands at your side and look down as if admiring your clothes.)

To have fun! (Put your hands up high as if you are cheering.)

Say the Stand up chant (see page 10). Divide the class into five groups. Give each group a piece of paper showing a number from 1–5. Repeat each line of the song. When the song says 'Number 1', point to the group with the number 1 paper and model how to mime putting on trousers.

Do the same with each number. Then, repeat the song line by line again, helping each group to notice when it is their turn. Next, practise with the audio using the same process but without pausing.

Have each group pass their paper to another group and play the song again. Repeat three more times until each group has had a chance to mime putting on the different items of clothing.

🍃 Table time

Say the Table time chant (see page 11).

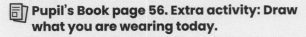

Pupil's Book page 55. Worksheet 5: Count, match and trace.

Show pupils page 55 and walk around to check that everyone is on the correct page. Say *Let's count the boots, one, two. Where's the number 2?* Move your finger over the numbers. Say *Here it is! Let's draw a line.* Show how to draw a line from the boots to the correct number. Continue to model the other answers, or, if you think pupils can complete the activity independently, say *Draw the lines.* Then point to the numbers and say *1, 2, 3, 4, 5. Let's trace the numbers.* Show how to follow the arrows do this. Monitor and help pupils as needed.

🍃 Goodbye

Follow the description on page 9.

🍃 Extra activities

Pupil's Book page 56. Extra activity: Draw what you are wearing today.

Say *What are you wearing, (Lucía?) Let's see, trousers, shoes and a jumper.* Repeat with two other pupils. Say *What am I wearing?* (Describe, then draw your clothes in your book or on the board.) Say *Draw your clothes.* Monitor pupils and help as needed. Optional: have pupils share and describe their drawings to the class.

Do a number dictation.

Give each pupil a piece of a paper divided into four sections with each section numbered with a number from 1–4. Point to the space numbered 1, say *Point to number 1. Number 1: draw two boots.* (Show how to do this on your own paper.) *Number 2: draw one dress. Number 3: draw two coats. Number 4: draw four hats.* Repeat each sentence several times and mime to give clues for vocabulary.

Teacher Resources Worksheet 17: Look and draw.

Pass out the worksheets, or ask your helper. Show pupils a sample worksheet for row 1. Trace the zig-zag lines with your finger and say *two* for the first jumper and *three* for the second one, counting as you trace each line with your finger. Continue in this way until you reach the fifth picture. Repeat the series so children can hear it again *One, two lines, one, two, three lines, one, two lines, one, two, three lines,* etc. *How many lines? One, two! Let's draw them.* Model how to trace one zig-zag line and draw in the other one. Repeat this process with the next row.

📝 Activity Book page 26 – Feel

Review clothes and different types of weather, including *hot* and *cold*. Hold up flashcards of different clothes for pupils to say if they wear them when it's hot or cold.

Ask pupils if they play outside when it's cold and what clothes they wear in cold weather. Use the pictures in the book to teach *scarf* and *gloves*.

Direct pupils' attention to the boy's hat in each picture of the book and have them notice what's different. Pupils first find and point to the other four differences, then circle all the differences in pencil.

🙆 **I make good decisions.** In L1, ask if the children in the second picture are wearing good clothes for cold weather. Elicit that they are. Pupils can then assess the weather where they are, and decide what they need to put on to go and play outside. Say *Well done – a (hat and coat). That's a good idea.* Pupils then repeat the affirmation *I make good decisions* with you.

☺ **Now you!** Give pupils some free time to play outside in the clothes they chose.

🌱 Help pupils to appreciate the seasons. In L1, talk about the seasons you have in your country and how the natural landscape changes in different seasons. Ask what activities they can do in each season and take a class vote on what season they like best.

Lesson 6

Lesson objective
To consolidate all unit content.

Language
Review: numbers *1–5*; clothes; Big Book language structures
Receptive: *It's your turn. Roll the dice. Find and stick.*

Materials
Presentation Plus, Greenman Puppet, Big Book story Unit 4, PB page 57, Flashcards Units 1–4, Class Audio, Stickers Unit 4, big dice, crayons, pencils. Optional: AB page 27

 Use Presentation Plus to play the games.

Consolidation
WORKSHEET 6

Find, stick and say.

Name

57

🍃 Starting the lesson

Settle the class with an opening routine (see Teacher's Book pages 8 and 9).

🍃 Active time

Warmer

Review Flashcards from Units 1–4 by holding each one up and saying the vocabulary words with the pupils and having them do each gesture or movement. You may wish to use the audio of the Unit 4 vocabulary to review (Track 35).

Game: *Roll, jump and say*

Follow the description on page 19.

🍃 Story review

Say the Story time chant (see page 10) and motion opening a book. Reread the story, while inviting the pupils to participate in saying the words or lines that they know.

▷ Alternatively, you may want to play the story video.

🍃 Table time

Say the Table time chant (see page 11).

Pupil's Book page 57. Worksheet 6: Find, stick and say.

Help the pupils to find page 57 in the Pupil's Book and locate the stickers for Unit 4. Say *Find and stick the pictures.* Have Greenman repeat each word several times as pupils look for the correct sticker to put in each place. Monitor the children as they work, and encourage them along, or give gesture clues. Repeat with each vocabulary word. When they have finished, have pupils point to each sticker and say the word.

🍃 Goodbye

Follow the description on page 9.

📖 Activity Book page 27 – Care

Review the clothes vocabulary and, in L1, talk about growing too big for our clothes. Elicit ideas for what we can do with our clothes when we've outgrown them. Show or draw a picture of a small hat and ask pupils to suggest other things it could be used for, e.g. to carry things, a hat for a teddy, etc.

Show pupils the activity in the book and talk about how the boots are being reused. Give them time to draw their own ideas for a welly boot garden in the empty boot on the page.

Pupils then think of what they could draw on the T-shirt (to upcycle it and turn it into a piece of wall art).

🙌 **I have good ideas.** Compare pupils' ideas for upcycling the T-shirt. Say *You have lots of good ideas. Well done!* Pupils repeat the affirmation *I have good ideas* with you.

☺ **Now you!** Ask pupils to bring in an old item of clothing to upcycle in a future lesson. They can do this in an indoor or outdoor classroom. Alternatively, bring in some cardboard packets, boxes and tubes for them to upcycle.

🌱 Help pupils understand the importance of reusing things to reduce waste and protect nature.

To end the unit, pupils can circle the bird on page 3.

Extra Phonics Lesson

Lesson objective
To introduce two new phonics sounds (long 'oo' as in 'moon' and short 'oo' as in 'cook').

Language
New: *cook, moon*

Materials
Presentation Plus, Greenman Puppet, PB page 58, downloadable Phonics Flashcards, Class Audio, pencils.
Optional: Teacher Resources Worksheet 18, scissors, glue sticks

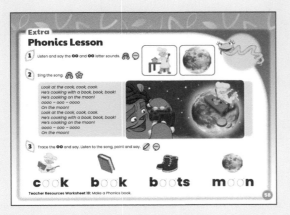

🔊 Phonics time

Warmer

Show children the *oo* (moon) and (cook) Phonics Flashcards on Presentation Plus. Read the words, then segment the sounds. Say *Look at the picture: There is a moon. Listen to the sound: oo. Listen and repeat: m-o-ooon.* Repeat with the second sound. Point to the Phonics Flashcards and segment the sounds three times, asking different pupils to repeat after you.

📖 Pupil's Book page 58. 1. Listen and say the *oo* and *oo* letter sounds.

Have pupils repeat the words again after Greenman. Hold both hands up making a circle to show *moon*. Pretend to hold a bowl and stir for *cook*. Repeat the sounds emphasising the short *oo* in *cook*, and the long *oo* in *moon*. Play the audio and have pupils listen and say the sounds and words. Repeat three times.

oo – oo – oo	cook
oo – oo – oo	moon

📖 Pupil's Book page 58. 2. Sing the song.

Show pupils the picture in activity 2. Play the song. Point to items in the picture to help pupils understand meaning. After playing the

track three times, say it slowly, and have pupils repeat each line, while looking at the picture. Introduce some gestures for pupils to follow. Continue repeating until pupils are saying at least the *oooo-ooo-oooo* and *cook, cook, cook* parts of the song, and are showing some comprehension through gestures.

🎧 **41** *Look at the cook, cook, cook.*
(Pretend to look through binoculars, aiming upwards.)
He's cooking with a book, book, book!
(Pretend to stir a pot with one hand, show the open palm of your other hand to indicate looking at a book.)
He's cooking on the moon! (Pretend to stir a pot, hold hands in a circle to make a moon.)
Oooo – ooo – oooo
On the moon! (Hold hands in a circle to make a moon.)

📖 Pupil's Book page 58. 3. Trace the *oo* and say. Listen to the song, point and say.

Show pupils activity 3 in your book. Say *Look at the oo-oo-oo, let's trace the letters! Cook, book, boots, moon.* Model following the arrows to complete the letters. Monitor pupils as they work. Then have them point to each word and say it after you. Play the song again and model how to point to the picture when you hear that word. Pause the song and have pupils repeat it, emphasising the target sound. Ask pupils if they know which word is not in the song (*boots*).

🔊 Extra activities

Teacher Resources Worksheet 18: Make a Phonics book.

Prepare one worksheet for each pupil in advance. Review the *oo* letter sounds and the words, *cook* and *boots*. Using an example worksheet, model how to trace over the dashed lines to complete the pictures. Monitor as the pupils do this and then let them colour the pictures. Model how to cut out both parts of the book (the inner part and the front and back cover). Show the pupils your complete mini book as an example and model how to stick the back of the cover, *My book*, onto the back of the *hoot* page and the back of *boots*, onto the back of the *cooks* page. Show the pupils how to fold the paper in half to make the book. Read the book as a class. Have the pupils repeat the words after you, emphasising the difference between the short and long *oo* sounds.

Winter fun!

Lesson objective

To review vocabulary from Units 3 and 4 and sing a song about winter.

Language

New: *snowman*

Review: *white; cold, rainy, snowy, windy;* the body and clothes

Receptive: *jumping, running, walking; Where does the (hand) go? Let's draw a line.*

Materials

Presentation Plus, Greenman Puppet, PB page 59, Flashcards Units 3 and 4, Class Audio, crayons, pencils. Optional: Teacher Resources Worksheets 19 and 20, paints, scissors, glue sticks

🐦 Starting the lesson

Settle the class with an opening routine (see Teacher's Book pages 8 and 9).

🐦 Active time

Warmer

Review weather vocabulary (you can use the Routine Boards on Presentation Plus to do this). Pupils can choose the vocabulary that is most appropriate for winter. Have the pupils use gestures to show the different types of weather. (Pretend to pick up snow and throw it in the air for *snowy*, blow out air and move your hands in swirling motions for *windy*, and shiver, saying 'brrr' to show *cold*.)

Say the vocabulary.

Have Greenman hold up each of the Flashcards from Units 3 and 4. Have the pupils say (or repeat) each word. Gradually speed up, so pupils have to try to identify the words as quickly as possible.

A winter's day song: Sing and do the actions.

Say *It's cold! What do we do?* Pretend to blow on your hands to keep warm. Say *We can put on our …* (act out putting on a hat and elicit the vocabulary word). Do the same with a coat. Now, act as if you've just found snow on the classroom floor. Say *It's white snow! Ooh, it's very cold!* Gesture for the pupils to pick up some imaginary snow as well.

Play the song once and model the actions. Then have the pupils join in as you say the song line by line and do the actions with them. Repeat this until most pupils are saying some of the words and participating in the actions. Then play the audio again, modelling the actions for the pupils to join in. Repeat the song until the class is singing most of the words and doing the actions.

 A winter's day

Walking in the forest on a winter's day. (Walk in place.)

It's cold and it's rainy, that's OK. (Wrap your arms around yourself like you're cold.)

We like winter and we can play. (Pretend to pick up snow and throw it in the air.)

Rainy fun on a winter's day! (Pretend to put on a hat and gloves.)

Running in the forest on a winter's day. (Run in place.)

It's cold and it's windy, that's OK. (Wrap your arms around yourself like you're cold.)

We like winter and we can play. (Pretend to pick up snow and throw it in the air.)

Windy fun on a winter's day!
(Pretend to put on a coat and gloves.)

Jumping in the forest on a winter's day.
(Jump in place.)

It's cold and it's snowy, that's OK. (Wrap your arms around yourself like you're cold.)

We like winter and we can play.
(Pretend to pick up snow and throw it in the air.)

Snowy fun on a winter's day!
(Pretend to put on a hat and gloves.)

Winter's fun on a winter's day.
(Pretend to pick up snow and throw it in the air.)

Table time

Say the Table time chant (see page 11).

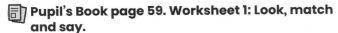 Pupil's Book page 59. Worksheet 1: Look, match and say.

Show pupils page 59 and walk around to check that everyone is on the correct page. Say *Where are the children?* Show pupils how to point to the photo of the children. Say *Where's the clothes shop?* Show pupils how to point to the shop. Say *Where does the hand go? Let's draw a line.* Model how to draw a line from the hand to the children. Repeat the process with the other pictures, matching the parts of the body to the photo of the children and the clothes to the clothes shop. Pupils may be able to work independently on this. Review the activity as a class, saying *What have the children got?* or *What's in the clothes shop?* Have pupils say the correct answers together.

Note: Pupils may wish to match some of the clothes to the photo of the children, too. If they do, encourage them to point out the items of clothing that match, e.g. the hat and the boy's hat in the photo.

Goodbye

Follow the description on page 9.

Extra activities

Pupil's Book page 60. Extra activity: Trace and colour the snowman.

Help pupils to find the correct page in the Pupil's Book. Use the picture to present the word *snowman*. Have pupils trace a circle in the air. Say *Let's make a circle with our fingers, let's make one more circle in the air. Now let's use our pencils to draw a circle for the snowman!* Model how to trace the lines for each circle of the snowman. Pupils may colour when they have finished tracing. Monitor as the pupils work.

Game: *Choose a card*

Have pupils sit in a circle. Spread the Flashcards from Units 3 and 4 face down in the centre. Model the activity yourself first. Turn over a card and say the word. Choose a pupil and, say (Lucía), *it's your turn. Choose a card.* Help the pupil to turn over the card, and say the word for them to repeat, if necessary. Play again until several pupils have had a turn. (Optional: you could also add the actions for each word.)

Teacher Resources Worksheets 19 and 20: Paint, cut and stick to make a winter scene.

Prepare the winter project worksheets for each pupil in advance. Play the *A winter's day* song (Track 42) again. Hold up Worksheet 19 and say *Let's make a winter scene!* Show the pupils Worksheet 20 and say *Point to the cloud. Point to Greenman. Point to Sam. Point to Nico. Point to the tree. Point to the snow. Point to the snowman. Now let's paint!* Model how to paint the winter background on Worksheet 19 and the individual pictures on Worksheet 20. Once the pupils have finished, they can cut out the pictures from Worksheet 20. Say *Let's make our winter scene! Let's put a snowman on the scene.* Model how to stick the snowman on the winter scene. Repeat with all the pictures from Worksheet 20. Say the words as you stick them to the background and encourage the pupils to repeat each word after you say it. Make a winter display with the worksheets.

Unit 5: Can I help you?

Lesson 1

Lesson objective
To introduce the main vocabulary for the unit (farm animals).

Language
New: *cow, hen, horse, pig, rabbit, sheep*
Review: *Hello, (Cow).* colours
Receptive: *Guess the word. What colour is the (pig)?*

Materials
Presentation Plus, Greenman Puppet, Big Book story Unit 5, PB page 61, Flashcards Units 1–5, Class Audio, crayons, pencils. Optional: PB page 62, AB page 28

 Use Presentation Plus to watch the unit introduction video and vocabulary song video. ▷

5 **Can I help you?**

Name

61

🍃 Starting the lesson

Settle the class with an opening routine (see Teacher's Book pages 8 and 9).

🍃 Active time

Welcome to Unit 5

▷ Tell pupils that you are about to start a new unit. Play the Unit 5 introduction video to introduce the unit topic. Pause the video at different points and ask, in L1, what the children can see and what they think they will learn about in this unit.

Warmer

Have Greenman take out the Units 1–4 Flashcards. Help the pupils do the actions and say the words.

Game: *Guess the word*

Have Greenman take out the Unit 5 Flashcards. Say *What's this Greenman, new words?* Act very excited about the new words. Take each flashcard out individually and say *Look! A (cow)! Repeat, class, a (cow)! What is it? (A cow.)* While you say the word, use gestures to reinforce the concept. Repeat this process with each card.

Say *Let's practise! Guess the word.* Cover a card with your hand or a cloth and slowly uncover it. Pupils try to name it before it's uncovered. Repeat the process with each card and go through the game three or four times, or until the pupils are identifying the cards quite easily.

At this point, you may wish to use the audio of the unit vocabulary to listen and repeat as a class.

 cow, hen, horse, pig, rabbit, sheep

Farm animal rap: Rap and do the actions.

While pupils remain standing, play the *Farm animal* rap for the class. Hold up the flashcard when that animal is mentioned in the rap. Encourage pupils to use their actions to express the animal. Next, say the rap line by line, slowly, enunciating the words and doing the song actions. Then, repeat the audio three times, or until most pupils are participating in the actions and saying some of the words.

Farm animal

Hello, Cow. How are you?
(Wave 'hello', put your hands up with palms facing upward.)

Very well, thank you!
(Nod your head, do a thumbs up.)

I speak English, what about you? (Move your hand like a puppet talking, point to another person.)

I say moo, moo, moo, moo, moo, moo …!
(Pretend to chew slowly like a cow.)

Repeat with:

Horse – neigh (Shake your mane.)

Sheep – baa (Fluff your fluffy wool.)

Hen – cluck (Move your arms like a hen's wings.)

Pig – snort (Scrunch up your nose like a snout.)

Rabbit – sniff (Wiggle your nose like a rabbit.)

▷ You may wish to watch the vocabulary song video at this point.

🗨 Story time

Say the Story time chant *It's story time, story time, open the Big Book and look inside* and motion opening a book.

Open the Big Book to the first two pages of the Unit 5 story. Say *What do we see? Oh, look! A (cow)!* Encourage pupils to repeat the words and do the actions/noises. After identifying all of the vocabulary words, close the book.

🗨 Table time

Say the Table time chant (see page 11).

📑 **Pupil's Book page 61. Worksheet 1: Listen, colour and say.**

Show pupils page 61 in the Pupil's Book and walk around to check that everyone is on the correct page. Play the *Farm animal* rap (Track 44) again and show pupils how to point to each animal when it is mentioned in the rap. Make sure each child has a pink, brown, black and red crayon. Then say *We need to colour the animals. What colour is the pig?* Elicit the response *pink* and tell the pupils to find the pink crayon and colour in the pig. Then say *Colour the horse brown. Colour the cow black and white. Colour the sheep black. Colour the rabbit brown. Colour the hen red.* Then have them point to each animal and say the word.

🗨 Goodbye

Follow the description on page 9.

Extra activities

📑 **Pupil's Book page 62. Extra activity: Draw and colour your favourite farm animal.**

Hold up the Unit 5 Flashcards. Say *Which animal do you like, (Lucía)?* Hold up different flashcards for the pupil to choose an animal from. Go around the class, asking pupils to choose. Then say *Draw your favourite animal.* Monitor the pupils as they work.

Optional: have pupils share their pictures with the class, and say the colours they chose for their animal.

Game: *Guess the animal*

Make an animal noise. Say *What is it?* Pupils will guess the animal (offer help with flashcards). Do this with various animal noises. Then, have a pupil take over your role. Give several pupils a turn to make the animal noise.

📝 Activity Book page 28 – Observe

Review farm animals and the forest animals that pupils know. Pupils can then walk around the class pretending to be the different animals.

Draw pictures of animal footprints on the board, or use photos of footprints, and ask pupils to guess the animals that made the footprints.

Draw pupils' attention to the footprints in the book and have them guess what animals they belong to. They trace the trails with their fingers or a pencil from left to right to find the answer, then colour the animal. There is no animal after the final set of footprints. Elicit that they belong to a horse and have pupils draw a horse in the box.

🙆 **I look carefully.** Praise pupils for looking so carefully and matching the footprints with the animals correctly. Remind pupils how important it is to take time to look around carefully and learn from our surroundings. Pupils repeat the affirmation *I look carefully* with you.

☺ **Now you!** Pupils can keep a look out for animal tracks when out on walks with their parents as a home-school connection activity. Alternatively, take the class out for a walk in school time. Encourage pupils to think about the best places to look, e.g. muddy puddles, sandpits and wet concrete. If they can't find any footprints, they can have fun making their own footprints in the mud!

🌿 Help pupils understand that animals share the world with us, and that we can look for signs they are there without seeing the animals themselves. Pupils can learn to appreciate the importance of animals in the world and how we need to protect their habitats.

Lesson 2

Lesson objective
To present the key structures for the unit.

Language
New: *Have you got (strong wings)? Yes, I have. No, I haven't. Can you (fly)? Yes, I can. No, I can't. orange, grey; spikes;* farm animals
Review: *bird, hedgehog;* colours
Receptive: *Which animal is this? Draw a line.*

Materials
Presentation Plus, Greenman Puppet, Big Book story Unit 5, PB page 63, Flashcards Unit 5, Class Audio, homemade bird and orange and grey hedgehog pictures, pencils.
Optional: PB page 64, Teacher Resources Worksheet 21, scissors, glue sticks, AB page 29

 Use Presentation Plus to watch the story video. ▷

Name _____ 63

☙ Starting the lesson

Settle the class with an opening routine (see Teacher's Book pages 8 and 9).

☙ Active time

Warmer

Review the vocabulary using the Unit 5 Flashcards.

Answer the questions.

Have Greenman ask you *Have you got (strong legs)?* Say *Yes, I have!* Show that your legs are strong by stretching and jumping. Have Greenman ask *Have you got (strong arms)?* Say *Yes, I have!* Show your muscles to show your strong arms. Ask the class these questions. Have them show you their strong arms and legs as they answer. Repeat with different parts of the body. Then make your arms hang loose at your sides with hunched over shoulders. Have Greenman ask you *Have you got (strong arms)?* again. This time, shake your head sadly and say *No, I haven't.* Repeat with legs and then ask the class these questions.

Now have Greenman ask *Can you fly?* Look at your arms and try to flap them. Say *No, I can't.* Have Greenman ask you *Can you run?* Run in place and say *Yes, I can.* Ask the class these questions and have them do the actions as they answer.

☙ Story time

Say the Story time chant *It's story time, story time, open the Big Book and look inside* and motion opening a book.

Open the Big Book to the Unit 5 story. Ask about the animals and things on the page. Use the picture of Hedgehog on page

34 to present the colours *grey* and *orange* and introduce the word *spikes*. Have pupils come up and point to the different animals when you say them and then have the class make the animal noises.

Read the story or play the audio version (Track 45), pausing to use facial and hand gestures to help convey meaning.

▷ Alternatively, you may want to play the story video.

 ## Can I help you?

Hedgehog is in the forest.
'I'm sad. Where are my friends?' says Hedgehog.
'There's the farm. I can see my friends!'

'Hello, Bird,' says Hedgehog.
'Hello, Hedgehog,' says Bird.
'Can I help you?'
'Can you fly?'
'No, I can't.'
'Have you got strong wings?'
'No, I haven't.'
'I'm sorry. You can't help me.'
'OK. Bye bye!'

'Hello, Horse,' says Hedgehog.
'Hello, Hedgehog,' says Horse.
'Can I help you?'
'Can you run?'
'No, I can't.'
'Have you got strong legs?'
'No, I haven't.'

'I'm sorry. You can't help me.'
'OK. Bye bye!'

'Hello, Rabbit. It's smelly!' says Hedgehog.
'Hello, Hedgehog,' says Rabbit.
'Can I help you?'
'Can you jump?'
'No, I can't.'
'Have you got strong arms?'
'No, I haven't.'
'I'm sorry. You can't help me.'
'OK. Bye bye!'

'Hello, Greenman.'
'Hello, Hedgehog. What's the matter?'
'I can't help Bird, Horse or Rabbit. I can't fly, run or jump.'
'But you are strong! You are special! You have got strong spikes!'

'I am strong! I can help!' says Hedgehog.
'Well done, Hedgehog!' says Greenman.
'Thank you, Hedgehog!' says Rabbit.

Do a role-play.

Prepare a drawing of an orange and grey hedgehog and a bird before the class, and have the flashcards of a rabbit and horse ready. Divide the class into four groups and give each group one of the cards/pictures. Say the lines from the Unit 5 Big Book story. Encourage the groups to repeat the lines of their character after you. Break the lines up into small parts and use gestures to help convey meaning.

Have each group pass their card/picture to a different group and repeat the role-play.

🔊 Table time

Say the Table time chant (see page 11).

📖 Pupil's Book page 63. Worksheet 2: Find, match and say.

Show pupils page 63 and walk around to check that everyone is on the correct page. Point to each picture of an animal shown above and below the farm picture and elicit the word/say the word for the pupils to repeat. Now point to the bigger picture in the middle, say *Oh no, the animals are hiding!* Gesture 'hiding' by putting your hands over your face like 'peek-a-boo'. Say *Which animal is this?* Point to the cow's leg. Elicit the response *Cow.* Say *Very good, let's draw a line to the cow.* Draw a line in your own book as an example. Repeat with the other animals until the pupils understand the activity and can continue working independently. Monitor their work.

🔊 Goodbye

Follow the description on page 9.

🔊 Extra activities

📄 Pupil's Book page 64. Extra activity: Colour Hedgehog.

Hold up a picture of Hedgehog from the Big Book. Say *What colour is Hedgehog? His body is* (pause) *orange. His spikes are* (pause) *grey. Where's your grey crayon? Where's your orange crayon?* Pause for pupils to find and hold up the correct crayons. Show pupils page 64 and check that everyone is on the correct page. Say *Let's colour Hedgehog.*

Teacher Resources Worksheet 21: Trace, cut and match.

Pass out the worksheets or ask your helper. Point to the first animal. Say *It's a head! A horse head! Where are the legs? Where are the horse legs? Oh no!* Have pupils trace and then cut out the parts. Say *Let's make a horse-bird!* Have pupils match the horse head and bird body together. Repeat this with different funny animals. Pupils can choose their favourite new animals and colour the two halves the same colour.

Volunteers can act out their favourite new animals. Ask *Have you got (strong legs)?* to guess who they are.

📝 Activity Book page 29 – Find and make

Pupils find natural materials and use them to make a collage picture of an animal. Pupils can find some of the natural materials outside, either before or during the lesson, or, alternatively, bring the materials to class for pupils to find. Pupils will need to find leaves, flowers, acorns, stones and grasses.

Review animals pupils know. Then use the individual pictures in the book to talk about the different natural materials in English and L1. Point to the animal collage in the book and tell pupils they are going to make one, using the natural materials. Direct pupils' attention to how the natural materials are used to make the collage.

Pupils look for the natural materials, either outside or among the materials that have been brought to the classroom. When they find one of the items in the pictures, they can circle it.

🙂 **Now you!** Pupils make their animal collages with the materials they find.

🙌 **I am creative.** Praise pupils for their animal collages and say *They are so interesting.* Tell pupils they are creative because they have used their ideas to make such interesting animals. Pupils repeat the affirmation *I am creative* with you.

🌱 Encourage pupils to return any items they found outdoors after they have made their collages (they should arrange the items rather than stick them down) – and help them understand that some of the items are seeds (acorns), or they provide goodness for the soil (flowers, grass and leaves).

Lesson 3

Lesson objective

To introduce a contrasting concept (strong/weak), and a value (having self-confidence).

Language

New: *strong/weak; grey, orange; farm animals*
Review: *good/naughty, up/down, clean/dirty, big/small; colours*
Receptive: *Show me (strong arms). Has the (sheep) got (strong legs)? What does (Horse) have? Colour (Horse's legs).*

Materials

Presentation Plus, Greenman Puppet, PB page 65, Flashcards Unit 5, Pop-outs Unit 5, 6 craft sticks per pupil, sticky tape, Class Audio, crayons, pencils.
Optional: PB page 66, Teacher Resources Worksheet 22, AB page 30

 Use Presentation Plus to do the activity.

Name _____ 65

🍃 Starting the lesson

Settle the class with an opening routine (see Teacher's Book pages 8 and 9).

🍃 Active time

Warmer

Listen to the *Farm animal* rap (Track 44) again and encourage pupils to do the actions.

Game: *Greenman says*

Say *Greenman says, 'Show me strong arms.'* Make a muscle with your arms. Say *Greenman says, 'Show me weak arms.'* Let your arms hang weakly. Repeat with strong/weak legs (jump and stretch/slump your legs down), strong/weak wings (make pretend wings and flap them quickly/make limp wings that don't move). Play the game again, but this time tell pupils that if you don't say *Greenman says*, they shouldn't move. You can speed up the instructions to make the game more challenging.

Do a concepts review.

Call out the different contrasting concepts from this unit and the previous units: *good/naughty, up/down, clean/dirty, big/small, strong/weak*. Remind pupils how to do the gestures for each concept by modelling the actions as you say the words.

Review the concepts by saying the words and having pupils show you the action. Say *Show me 'up'. Very good! Show me 'down'. Well done!* Continue with each pair of contrasting concepts.

Good/naughty (Thumbs up/thumbs down.)

Up/down (Raise your hands up high over your head/squat down and touch your toes.)

Clean/dirty (Pretend to 'wash' your hands and then smile/look at your hands and then scrunch your nose and look away.)

Big/small (Stretch your arms wide at your sides/hold the index finger and thumb of each hand together to make a very small shape in front of you.)

Strong/weak (Make muscles with your arms/let your arms hand at your sides and hunch your shoulders over.)

🍃 Story time

Say the Story time chant *It's story time, story time, open the Big Book and look inside* and motion opening a book.

Take out the Big Book to show parts of the story where we can see each animal that Hedgehog offers to help. Say *Who's got strong (legs)? Yes, very good, (Horse). Who's got weak (legs)? Yes, Hedgehog's got weak (legs).* Be sure to use the actions for strong and weak and point to the parts of the body to make the message clear.

Reread the story or listen to the audio (Track 45).

▷ You may also choose to use the story video, pausing the video rather than pointing to pictures.

🍃 Table time

Say the Table time chant (see page 11).

Do the pop-out activity.

Direct pupils' attention to the pop-outs you have prepared: puppets of a horse, a sheep, a pig, a hen, a rabbit and a cow. Point to each of the animals and say *What's this?* Help the pupils if they have trouble thinking of the words.

Show pupils how to take out the pop-out pieces for Unit 5, carefully. Observe as they do this and help as needed. When all the pupils have finished, say *Show me the cow.* Hold up your cow puppet for the class to see as an example. Say *Show me the pig.* Repeat with the other farm animals.

Give each pupil six craft sticks and six pieces of tape. Show pupils how to tape their craft stick onto the back of their pop-outs. When they have finished, have pupils hold up the different animals as you name them.

Play the audio for the *Farm animal* rap (Track 44) and have pupils hold up their puppets when the different animals are mentioned in the rap. Give the class time to play with their puppets at the end. Circulate and ask, e.g. *Has the (sheep) got (strong legs)?* Remind pupils how to put away their pop-outs.

Pupil's Book page 65. Worksheet 3: Colour the strong parts.

Show pupils page 65 in the Pupil's Book and walk around to check that everyone is on the correct page. Say *What does Horse have? Strong …* Point to your own legs to elicit the response *legs.* Say *Colour Horse's legs.* Repeat the process with the other pictures (Hedgehog's spikes, Rabbit's arms and Bird's wings).

🍃 Goodbye

Follow the description on page 9.

🍃 Extra activities

Pupil's Book page 66. Extra activity: Trace and colour Greenman.

Help pupils to find page 66 in the Pupil's Book. Say *Look at Greenman! He's so strong! He's got strong arms!* (pause) *Let's trace the lines on Greenman.* Model how to trace the lines with a pencil. When the pupils have finished, say *Now let's colour Greenman. What colours do we need?* Hold up Greenman and elicit the colours *brown* and *green.* Say *OK, colour Greenman brown and green.* Monitor the pupils as they work.

Emotions: Feeling sad

Look at the part of the story where Hedgehog is talking to Greenman and ask *Is Hedgehog happy or sad?* Elicit that he is feeling sad. Encourage pupils to share when they feel sad and what makes them feel better.

Value activity: Having self-confidence

Introduce the concept with the Big Book story. Point to each animal and point out again their 'strong' part. Say *And you?*

Are you strong? Can you jump? Show me! Yes, you can, well done! Repeat this several times with different actions (run, sing, jump, dance, etc.). Go round the circle and have each pupil repeat something s/he can do, e.g. *I can dance.* At the end, point out that we are good at different things and differences are good!

Teacher Resources Worksheet 22: Draw three things you are good at.

Pass out the worksheets or ask your helper. Hold up a sample worksheet. Say *In the story, Rabbit can jump and he can pick up rubbish with his strong arms. Hedgehog has got strong spikes. He can pick up rubbish with his spikes. What can you do?* Elicit some ideas. Then show an example worksheet with pictures of three things you can do. Say *I can (run, jump and dance). Draw three things you can do.*

📖✏️ Activity Book page 30 – Investigate

Review animals pupils know. Show them how to classify animals into *big* and *small*, and *strong* or *weak*.

Introduce the concept of a big/strong bridge and a small/weak bridge, using the picture in the book or by demonstrating the concept in the classroom. For example, pull two tables together and make a bridge between them. First, make quite a strong bridge, using something like a large hardback book. Show pupils how many things can be piled onto it, because it's a strong bridge. Then make a paper bridge, and ask pupils to guess if it can carry the same number of things. (No, – it's weak.)

Show pupils how to do the activity in the book. They choose and draw the animal that will have to cross the stream on the big, strong, bridge (the horse), then draw the smaller, lighter animal on the smaller, weaker bridge (the rabbit).

🙌 **I am clever.** Check that pupils have drawn the animals on the correct bridge. Say *Well done!* and remind them how clever they are for understanding how strong things can carry heavier weights. Pupils repeat the affirmation *I am clever* with you.

😊 **Now you!** Pupils can then go outside and make their own bridges, using sticks and other natural materials. Encourage them to find out which materials they can use to make the strongest bridge, and then test their strength with stones or sticks. Alternatively, they can make bridges in the classroom using books and pencils, and then test their strength with other classroom objects.

🌱 Help pupils understand that things are strong and weak in nature, and that they need to be careful when playing in nature. For example, they should never walk on frozen water because the ice may be too weak.

Lesson 4

Lesson objective
To use TPR to review unit vocabulary through an action song.

Language
New: *eat, fly, jump, move, run, sleep, walk;* farm animals
Review: colours
Receptive: *What does (Horse) do? Stop! Where's the (cow) shape? Let's draw a line.*

Materials
Presentation Plus, PB page 67, Flashcards Unit 5, picture of a bird, Class Audio, music, crayons, pencils. Optional: PB page 68, AB page 31

 Use Presentation Plus to watch the action song video. ▷

Name _____ 67

🍃 Starting the lesson

Settle the class with an opening routine (see Teacher's Book pages 8 and 9).

🍃 Active time

Warmer

Display the flashcards of *horse, rabbit, cow, hen* and *sheep* and a picture of a bird. Write the words *eat, fly, run, jump, walk* and *sleep* on the board and model an action for each. Have the pupils repeat each word. Then point to the picture of the bird and say *What does Bird do?* (Pause and do the *fly* action.) *Fly! What does Horse do?* (Pause and do the *run* action.) *Run!* Continue for Rabbit (*jump*), Cow (*eat*), Hen (*walk*) and Sheep (*sleep*).

Game: *Musical statues*

Say the Stand up chant (see page 10). Play this game using the actions introduced in the Warmer. First say and model each action and have the pupils practise for a short time. Repeat, but this time play music after saying the action. Every so often, pause the music and say *Stop!* Pupils must stand as still as statues in their pose. Anyone who moves helps you play the music again and call out the next action. Repeat each action various times.

I'm a little bird action song: Watch the video. Sing and do the actions.

▷ You may prefer to use the action song video to teach the pupils the actions and the song.

First, play the audio and hold up flashcards for the vocabulary words in the song. Invite the pupils to say the word when you hold up the card. The second time you play the song, do the actions to show the class. Next, have the pupils stand up. Teach them the actions one by one as you say each line of the song.

Practise the actions for the song three or four times slowly, going through the song line by line. Then, play the audio track and do the actions together. Repeat until all of the class is participating in each action and singing some of the words.

🎧 46 I'm a little bird

I'm a little bird, fly with me. (Move your hand like a beak, flap your imaginary wings.)

Move your wings, just like me. (Flap your imaginary wings.)

I'm a strong horse, run with me. (Shake your imaginary mane, run in place like a horse.)

Move your legs, just like me. (Run in place like a horse.)

I'm a white rabbit, jump with me. (Twitch your nose like a rabbit, jump in place.)

Move your feet, just like me. (Tap your feet, one at a time.)

I'm a hungry cow, eat with me. (Droop your eyelids, pretend to chew moving your jaw in a circular way like a cow.)

Move your mouth, just like me. (Pretend to chew moving your jaw in a circular way like a cow.)

I'm a happy hen, walk with me. (Walk like a hen.)

Move your head, just like me. (Move your head front to back like a hen.)

I'm a white sheep, sleep with me. (Bat your eyelids, put your hands under your head like a pillow.)

Close your eyes, just like me. (Close your eyes and pretend to sleep.)

🍃 Table time

Say the Table time chant (see page 11).

📑 Pupil's Book page 67. Worksheet 4: Look, match and say.

Show pupils page 67 in the Pupil's Book and walk around to check that everyone is on the correct page. Name each animal and its action: *Cow eats, Rabbit jumps, Hen walks, Sheep sleeps, Bird flies, Horse runs.* Say *Where's Cow?* Point to cow. *Oh, here she is. What does Cow do? Eat! Look, where's the cow shape?* Move your finger back and forth over the silhouettes on the page. Call on a volunteer to come up and point to the correct silhouette. Say *Well done. Let's draw a line.* Show how to draw a line from Cow to the correct silhouette. Continue with the other animals until pupils are prepared to work alone. Then, review the answers by having pupils trace a finger along the line between each animal and it's silhouette, as they say the word and the action.

🍃 Goodbye

Follow the description on page 9.

🍃 Extra activities

📑 Pupil's Book page 68. Extra activity: Say and colour the actions.

Help pupils to find the correct page in the Pupil's Book. Say *Find Bird. What does Bird do?* (pause) *(Fly!)* Act out flying movements. *Colour the flying bird!* Repeat with the other animals, saying the animal and eliciting its action, before pupils colour it.

Game: *Remember the cards*

See page 19 for a description of this game.

Listen and do.

Say an animal and have the pupils walk around and act like the animal, making that animal sound. Say *Be a (hen)!* and motion for pupils to act like a hen. Repeat with different animals, several times. Later, choose a volunteer to take over the teacher's role and choose which animal names to say for their classmates to act out.

 **Activity Book page 31 – Practise**

Review actions that pupils know, either by calling out actions for pupils to do on the spot or by repeating the action song from the Pupil's Book lesson (Track 46).

Direct pupils' attention to the questionnaire in the book and have them point to the different actions a cat *can* do. They then circle the five actions (*walk, run, jump, eat* and *sleep*). Have them point to the action a cat *can't* do (*fly*) and talk about why a cat can't do that. When they have completed, the questionnaire, pupils can colour the star at the bottom of the certificate.

You may wish to have the pupils complete the questionnaires for themselves, if appropriate.

☺ **Now you!** Pupils perform an exercise routine in the playground or another outdoor space, by acting out the different actions from the book.

🧘 **I can do it.** Praise pupils for completing the activity correctly and for doing the actions themselves. Pupils repeat the affirmation *I can do it* after doing each action.

🌱 Remind pupils how important it is to take exercise outside in the fresh air, as they improve their muscle strength and breathe fresh oxygen into their bodies.

Lesson ⑤

Lesson objective
To work on pre-writing skills and practise numbers through a song.

Language
New: *number 6; strong/weak; farm animals*
Review: *dirty/clean; colours; numbers 1–5*
Receptive: *Let's (clap). Point to the (strong) chick. Draw a line. Let's trace the numbers.*

Materials
Presentation Plus, PB page 69, Class Audio, crayons, pencils. Optional: PB page 70, Teacher Resources Worksheet 23, AB page 32

 Use Presentation Plus to do the activities and watch the Forest Fun Activity Book yoga video.

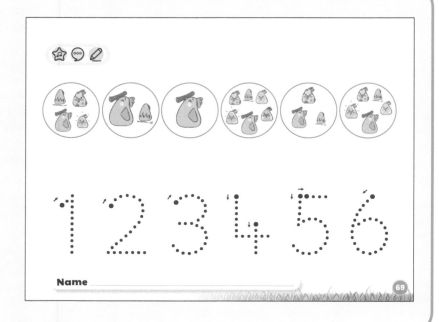

🍃 Starting the lesson

Settle the class with an opening routine (see Teacher's Book pages 8 and 9).

🍃 Active time

Warmer

Review numbers *1–5* and present the number *6* (you can use the Flashcards on Presentation Plus to do this).

Draw three chicks on the board and practise numbers by counting the chicks and the parts of the body. Say *How many chicks are there?* Count as a class *One, two, three. Three chicks.* Ask pupils *How many eyes are there? One, two, three, four, five six. Six eyes.* Continue counting other parts of the body (tummies, legs, wings).

Game: *Count and clap*

Practise saying numbers and having the pupils clap that number of times. Say *Let's clap one time, one* (clap once) *two* (clap twice). Continue to *six.* To begin with, clap along with the pupils. Once they are more confident in the activity, they can clap on their own. Continue the activity saying the numbers in random order. You may also choose to have a volunteer take over your role and say the numbers.

Six chicks number song 1–6: Sing and count.

Say *We know our numbers very well! Let's practise a song with them.* Have the pupils sit or stand and tell them to listen for numbers. Play the song holding up your fingers for the numbers.

Next, say the song line by line doing the actions. Do this three times, then play the audio again. Repeat until the pupils are singing many of the words, focusing on the number words.

 47 **Six chicks** 🎵

Mummy hen, (Flap your arms at your sides.)

Has got 6 chicks. (Hold up six fingers.)

1, 2, 3, 4, 5, 6. (Count on your fingers.)

1! – I'm strong. (Hold up one finger, make a muscle with your arm.)

2! – I'm weak. (Hold up two fingers, let your arm hang down.)

3! – I'm dirty. (Hold up three fingers, hold your hands in front of you to look at them, then wrinkle your nose and turn away.)

4! – I'm clean. (Hold up four fingers, hold your hands in front of you to look at them and act as if you are admiring them and smile.)

5! – I'm yellow. (Hold up five fingers.)

6! – I'm pink. (Hold up six fingers.)

1, 2, 3, 4, 5, 6 (Count on your fingers.)

🍃 Table time

Say the Table time chant (see page 11).

📑 Pupil's Book page 69. Worksheet 5: Count, match and trace.

Show pupils page 69 in the Pupil's Book and walk around to check that everyone is on the correct page. Hold up your own book and point out the different chicks. Review the contrasting concepts from this unit and Unit 3 by saying *Point to the strong chick.* (Point to the big orange chick holding a twig in its beak to show pupils it's the 'strong' one.) *Point to the weak chick.* (Point to the thin purple chick who has dropped the twig.) *Point to the clean chick,* (point to the green chick) *and the dirty chick.* (Point to the grey chick.) Repeat this several times until pupils have understood the concept. Continue with the colours, say *Point to the yellow chick, point to the pink chick.* Listen to the *Six chicks* song (Track 47) again and point to the chicks when you hear them mentioned in the song.

Next, point to the first circle with four chicks and say *Let's count the chicks in this circle. One, two, three, four! Four chicks! Let's find number 4. Now draw a line.* Show the pupils how to draw a line from the 4 to the circle with the four chicks. Let the pupils finish on their own. Then say *Let's trace the numbers 1–6.* Model in your book how to trace the numbers. Observe the pupils as they work. Then review the answers together as a class.

🍃 Goodbye

Follow the description on page 9.

🍃 Extra activities

📑 Pupil's Book page 70. Extra activity: Colour the six chicks.

Show pupils page 70 and walk around to check that everyone is on the correct page. Count the chicks together. Say *Let's count, one, two, three, four, five, six. Six chicks.* Say *One is strong.* (Make a muscle with your arm.) *What colour is strong?* Show pupils page 69 in your book to remind them, say *Yes, strong is orange. Let's colour.* Monitor as pupils colour the first chick orange. Then repeat this process with: two (weak – purple), three (dirty – grey), four (clean – green), five (yellow) and six (pink). Monitor and review the colours once all the pupils have finished.

Count the pupils.

Have pupils stand in a circle. Walk around putting pupils in groups of one to six. Say and motion *Stay together* and get them to hold hands. Count each pupil as you put them into groups. When you finish, count the pupils in each group again. The whole class participates in counting each group aloud.

Teacher Resources Worksheet 23: Trace Hedgehog.

Pass out the worksheet or ask your helper. Hold up a sample worksheet and say *Look at Hedgehog's spikes! He is strong! Let's count the spikes: one, two, three, four, five, six. Now, let's trace the spikes.* Model how to trace the lines of each spike.

✏️ Activity Book page 32 – Feel

Review parts of the body, and pre-teach the word *knees*, by asking pupils to touch their heads, toes, etc.

Teach the word *butterfly* by drawing a butterfly on the board. Direct pupils' attention to the children in their book. Explain they are doing the butterfly pose.

Pupils do the activity in the book. Show them how to trace, then draw, the butterflies' wings. They then draw draw their face onto the second child doing yoga, to personalize it. Allow time for pupils to colour the butterflies.

🙂 ▷ **Now you!** Have pupils do some stretching exercises with you. You can also review the yoga poses they already know from Units 1 and 3. Model how to do the butterfly pose and get pupils to copy you. Help pupils understand their legs are the butterfly wings. As they move them up and down, say *Look! We can fly!* Pupils can watch the video for more practise. They can also act out flying around the room as happy butterflies, as the children do in the video.

🧘 **I feel happy.** After you have finished the yoga activity, smile and say *I feel happy.* Ask pupils, in L1, if they feel happy too, and remind them that we often feel happy when we do yoga together. Encourage pupils to repeat the affirmation *I feel happy* with you.

🌱 Pupils can learn about a butterfly's life cycle, or about planting flowers that attract butterflies to gardens and wildlife spaces –such as buddleia, verbena or lavender. Pupils can also set up a homemade butterfly feeding centre in their playground, using sponges soaked in sugar solution.

Lesson 6

Lesson objective
To consolidate all unit content.

Language
Review: farm animals; Big Book language structures
Receptive: *What's that? Now you. Find and stick.*

Materials
Presentation Plus, Greenman Puppet, Big Book story Unit 5, PB page 71, Flashcards Units 1–5, Class Audio, Stickers Unit 5, sticky tape/tack, crayons, pencils. Optional: AB page 33

 Use Presentation Plus to play the games.

Starting the lesson

Settle the class with an opening routine (see Teacher's Book pages 8 and 9).

Active time

Warmer

Review Flashcards from Units 1–5 by holding each one up and saying the vocabulary word with the pupils. Say *What's this? Is it a (hand)?* (wait for pupils to respond) *Oh! It's a hen!* Exchange different vocabulary words and then confirm the correct answer. You may wish to use the audio of the Unit 5 vocabulary to review (Track 43).

Game: *Walk like the animals*

Tape or tack the Unit 5 Flashcards in different places around the room. When you say an animal, a pupil will walk to the flashcard, acting like that animal. First, go through the activity yourself so the pupils see an example. Point to the *hen* flashcard and say *What's that?* Help the pupils to respond *A hen.* Then move to the card flapping your imaginary wings, walking and moving your head from front to back. Come back to the circle. Say *Now you, (Lucía). A horse!* If the pupil acts unsure, do the action beside him/her along the way. Continue with different animals until all of the pupils have had a turn.

Story review

Say the Story time chant *It's story time, story time, open the Big Book and look inside* and motion opening a book.

Reread the story and invite the pupils to participate in saying the words or lines that they know.

▷ Alternatively, you may want to play the story video.

Table time

Say the Table time chant (see page 9).

Pupil's Book page 71. Worksheet 6: Find, stick and say.

Help the pupils to find page 71 in the Pupil's Book and locate the stickers for Unit 5. Say *Find and stick the pictures.* Have Greenman repeat each word several times as pupils look for the correct sticker to put in each place. Monitor children as they work and encourage them along, or give gesture clues. Repeat with each vocabulary word. When they have finished, have pupils point to each sticker and say the word.

Goodbye

Follow the description on page 9.

Activity Book page 33 – Care

Review the words for animals pupils know and, in L1, talk about the different food they eat.

Use some real grass or the picture in the book to elicit/teach the word *grass*. Pupils think and say which animals eat grass. Then ask them which animal the child on the page might be feeding and elicit some ideas. Pupils can draw this animal into the space.

I care for animals. Pupils share their pictures, and think about ways they are kind to pets and other animals. Praise them for their ideas. Then pupils repeat the affirmation *I care for animals* with you.

☺ **Now you!** Pupils can feed an animal at home – it could be a pet, or they may put out food for the birds or other wild creatures. Alternatively, pupils can put out food and water for birds at school.

Help pupils to understand it's important to look after wild animals, such as birds, as well as pets. Also get them to think about appropriate food for different animals.

To end the unit, pupils can circle the hedgehog on page 3.

Extra Phonics Lesson

Lesson objective
To Introduce two new phonics sounds ('sh' and 'ee').

Language
New: *bee*

Materials
Presentation Plus, PB page 72, downloadable Phonics Flashcards, Class Audio, crayons, pencils. Optional: Teacher Resources Worksheet 24, scissors, glue sticks

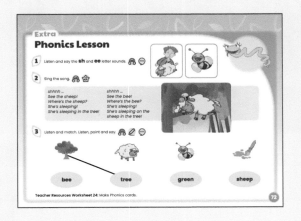

🖋 Phonics time

Warmer

Show children the *sh* and *ee* Phonics Flashcards. Read the words then segment the sounds. Say *Look at the picture: There is a sheep. Listen to the sound: sh. Listen and repeat: shh-h-h-h-h.* Repeat with the second sound. Point to the Phonics Flashcards and say the sounds three times, asking different pupils to repeat after you.

📖 Pupil's book page 72. 1. Listen and say the *sh* and *ee* letter sounds.

Say *Sh! The sheep is asleep.* (Put your finger to your lips.) *Point to the sheep. Point to the bee.* Say *Sh-sh-sh, ee-ee-ee.* Point to the correct pictures in your own book to give clues. Repeat the words in different orders and monitor to check pupils are pointing to the right pictures. Play the audio and have pupils listen and repeat the sounds and words. Repeat three times.

sh – sh – sh	shhhhhhhh!
ee – ee – ee	bee

📖 Pupil's book page 72. 2. Sing the song.

Show pupils the picture in activity 2. Play the song. Point to items in the picture to help pupils understand meaning. After playing the track three times, say it slowly, and have pupils repeat each line,

while looking at the picture. Introduce some gestures for pupils to follow. Continue repeating until pupils are saying at least the *She's sleeping* part of the song, and are showing some comprehension through gestures.

Shhhh … See the sheep! (Put index finger against your lips.)
Where's the sheep? (Make a questioning gesture.)
She's sleeping! (Palms together under tilted head in sleeping gesture.)
She's sleeping in the tree! (Continue sleeping gesture, make a tree shape with arms.)
Shhhh … See the bee! (Make a flying motion with hands.)
Where's the bee? (Make a questioning gesture.)
She's sleeping! (Palms together under tilted head in sleeping gesture.)
She's sleeping on the sheep in the tree! (Continue sleeping gesture, make a tree shape with arms.)

📖 Pupil's book page 72. 3. Listen and match. Listen, point and say.

Show pupils activity 3. Play the audio and pause after the first item. Point to the first picture. Say *What's this? Oh, yes, a tree. Where's the word for 'tree'?* Point to the word and picture. Help pupils to find the right word in their own books as you walk around. Say *Let's trace the line.* Model tracing the example line in the book with your finger. Repeat the same process with the other words and have pupils draw matching lines. Then play the audio again while pupils listen, point to the pictures and words and repeat.

See the tree	t – r – ee	tree
See the sheep	sh – ee – p	sheep
See the bee	b – ee	bee
See green	g – r – ee – n	green

🖋 Extra activities

Teacher Resources Worksheet 24: Make Phonics cards.

Prepare a worksheet for each pupil. Pupils will make three *ee* cards. Show the pupils a prepared example of the finished cards. Say *Let's cut out our Phonics cards.* Give pupils time to colour the pictures. Model how to cut out the cards and letters, then have pupils lay them out in a line on the desk. Say *Listen to the words and put the 'ee' sound in its place.* Say each word, *tree, bee,* and *sheep,* emphasising the *ee* sound. Go slowly, so that the pupils have time to stick the *ee* onto the words. Encourage them to say the words as they do this. When they have finished, they can colour the pictures.

Unit 6: The summer party

Lesson 1

Lesson objective

To introduce the main vocabulary for the unit (food).

Language

New: *carrot, egg, juice, plum, potato, sausage*
Review: colours; numbers *1–6*
Receptive: *What is it? Take out your (crayons).*

Materials

Presentation Plus, Greenman Puppet, Big Book story Unit 6, PB page 73, Flashcards Unit 6, Class Audio, crayons, pencils. Optional: PB page 74, plasticine or plastic food of the vocabulary items, picnic blanket, a box/bag/basket, AB page 34

Use Presentation Plus to watch the unit introduction video and vocabulary song video.

Starting the lesson

Settle the class with an opening routine (see Teacher's Book pages 8 and 9).

Welcome to Unit 6

Tell pupils that you are about to start a new unit. Play the Unit 6 introduction video to introduce the unit topic. Pause the video at different points and ask, in L1, what the children can see and what they think they will learn about in this unit.

Active time

Warmer

Present the Unit 6 Flashcards by holding them up and having Greenman say the words with the pupils.

Pass the cards and say.

Say the Circle time chant (see page 10). Have Greenman take out one flashcard and say the word, for example *juice.* He passes the card to the pupil on the right of you in the circle. Greenman says *Repeat, 'juice'.* Motion for the pupil to hand the card to the child on his right. Greenman says *What is it?* The pupil responds *juice.* The next pupil may be able to say the word without prompting.

Pass the card all the way around the circle, with each pupil saying the word. Then repeat the process with the remaining cards, one at a time.

At this point, you may wish to use the audio of the unit vocabulary to listen and repeat as a class.

51 *carrot, egg, juice, plum, potato, sausage*

Have you got an egg, please? song: Sing and do the actions.

While pupils remain standing, play the *Have you got an egg, please?* song for the class. Hold up a flashcard each time a food word is mentioned in the song. Next, say the song line by line, slowly, enunciating the words and doing the actions. Then, repeat the audio three times, or until most pupils are participating by doing the actions and singing some of the words.

52 **Have you got an egg, please?**

*Have you got **an egg**, please?* (Hold your hands out at your sides, elbows bent, palms up and move your hands as you sing to emphasise the rhythm of the words.)

Yes, I have. (Hands on hips and nod and smile.)

*Can I have **an egg**, please?* (Put your hands in front of you, palms together, fingertips pointing up, as if pleading.)

Yes, you can. (Pretend to hold out an egg.)

Repeat with: *a potato, a carrot, a sausage, a plum, some juice*

▷ You may wish to watch the vocabulary song video at this point.

🍂 Story time

Say the Story time chant *It's story time, story time, let's open the Big Book and look inside* and motion opening a book. Open the Big Book to page 48 of the Unit 6 story. Say *What do we see? Oh, look! A party! It's summer.* Elicit the words for items that pupils are familiar with in the picture (the characters, clothes, tree, etc.). After identifying all of the food vocabulary words, close the book.

🍂 Table time

Say the Table time chant (see page 11).

 Pupil's Book page 73. Worksheet 1: Look, colour and say.

Show pupils page 73 and walk around to check that everyone is on the correct page. Play the *Can I have an egg, please?* song (Track 52) again. Show the pupils how to point to each item in the picture while listening to the song. Repeat the song until most of the class is finding the objects and singing at least some of the words.

Have Greenman say *Oh no! Your pictures need colour! Take out your crayons.* Have pupils complete each of the uncoloured pictures while you chant the word and point to the picture in the Big Book. When they have finished, have them point to each item of food and say the word.

🍂 Goodbye

Follow the description on page 9.

🍂 Extra activities

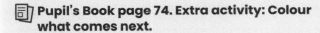 Pupil's Book page 74. Extra activity: Colour what comes next.

Draw a series of three colours on the board, or hold up something to represent each colour. Draw a spot of: red, blue, black, red, blue, black, red, blue, then two uncoloured circles. Say *Let's say the colours. Red, blue, black, red, blue, black, red, blue … What comes next? (Black.)* Say *Well done! What comes next? (Red.)* Say *Very good! Let's colour the sausage. Look at the book.* (Show the page and point to each sausage.) *Orange, brown, pink, orange, brown … What comes next? (Pink.) Let's colour the sausage pink. Get your pink crayon … colour!* Monitor the pupils as they work. Say *Now colour the next sausage. What colour is it? (Orange.) Good! Let's colour!*

Check pupils' work as you walk around.

Game: *Let's have a picnic!*

Prepare a cloth to use as a picnic blanket and some plasticine food items (or use plastic food) for the main vocabulary. Lay out your picnic blanket in the centre of the circle and begin to take the food items out of a box, bag or basket. Say *We're going to have a picnic! Let's eat a sausage,* (pause for pupils to repeat) *an egg,* (pause for pupils to repeat) *a potato,* (pause for pupils to repeat) *a carrot* (pause for pupils to repeat) *and a plum* (pause for pupils to repeat) *and drink juice* (pause for pupils to repeat). Review the foods by pointing to each item and encouraging the class to name it.

Pass an item to a pupil and say *What's this, (Lucía)?* They may need you to say each word for them to repeat. Continue passing the items to different pupils until most or all have had a turn.

📝 Activity Book page 34 – Observe

Use the pictures in the book to introduce the idea of a forest kitchen, where children make pretend food from materials around them in the forest. Ask pupils what forest foods the children are making. Review the word *cakes* and teach the word *soup.* Ask pupils to guess what the forest foods are made of and elicit ideas in English and L1.

Direct pupils' attention to the mud cakes in the first picture and count them together (there are five). Repeat with the second picture (there are six). Pupils find five more differences and then circle all the differences with a pencil.

☺ **Now you!** Ask pupils to think of different kinds of 'food' they could make in a forest kitchen. If you have access to an outdoor classroom, pupils could set up their own forest kitchen. Alternatively, they could draw some pictures of what they would make.

🙌 **I use my imagination.** Praise pupils for using their imagination and thinking of so many different ideas for a forest kitchen. Pupils repeat the affirmation *I use my imagination* with you.

🌱 Encourage pupils to use natural materials that are lying on the ground for their activities, rather than picking new materials. Teach pupils that they should tidy up after themselves and not leave any rubbish behind.

Lesson 2

Lesson objective
To present the key structures for the unit.

Language
New: *Have you got any (eggs)? Can I have some (eggs)? Here you are. I like sharing my (eggs).* food
Review: *Yes, I have. No, I haven't.* colours; numbers 1–6
Receptive: *Let's draw a line to the (eggs).*

Materials
Presentation Plus, Greenman Puppet, Big Book story Unit 6, PB page 75, Flashcards Unit 6, Class Audio, small hoop, plasticine, crayons, pencils. Optional: PB page 76, Teacher Resources Worksheet 25, scissors, paper fasteners, AB page 35

 Use Presentation Plus to watch the story video. ▷

Name _____

🍂 Starting the lesson

Settle the class with an opening routine (see Teacher's Book pages 8 and 9).

🍂 Active time

Warmer

Use the Unit 6 Flashcards to practise the unit vocabulary. Have Greenman hold up the flashcards and say the words for pupils to repeat.

Game: *The hoop game*

Follow the description on page 19.

Make plasticine food.

The pupils will use plasticine to make food. Before passing out plasticine to the class, model an example in front of them. Make a potato shape, hold up the potato flashcard and the plasticine shape together and say *Potato. Repeat, potato.*

Prepare to pass out a ball of plasticine to each pupil and say *One, two, three, hands on your knees.* Remind them that they should keep their hands on their knees until they have permission to begin making the food items you say.

When they have finished, choose a pupil to model a dialogue with you at the front of the class. Say *(Lucía), have you got any potatoes? (Lucía), say, 'Yes, I have.'* (The pupil repeats.) Say *Can I have some potatoes? (Lucía), say 'Yes, here you are.'* (The pupil repeats.) Gesture to show the pupil that he/she should give you his/her potato. Say *I like sharing my potatoes.* (The pupil repeats.)

Repeat this process with other pupils and items of plasticine food. Then, switch roles and whisper the question part of the dialogue to a pupil to repeat and ask you. Repeat with other pupils.

Walk around to collect the plasticine, congratulating each child.

🍂 Story time

Say the Story time chant *It's story time, story time, open the Big Book and look inside* and motion opening a book.

Look at the first pages of the story and point out the characters. Ask *Are they happy? No, they're sad! What happened?* Point to Fox sneaking away with the picnic food. Say *Oh no! Fox has got the food! Let's read the story.*

Read the story or play the audio version (Track 53), pausing to use facial and hand gestures to convey meaning. You may choose to have pupils repeat the lines practised in the dialogue *Have you got any (eggs)? Yes, I have. Can I have some (eggs), please?* and *I like sharing my (eggs). Here you are.*

▷ Alternatively, you may want to play the story video.

 The summer party

Sam, Nico and Greenman are in the forest.
'Hello, Sam. Hello, Nico. What are you doing?' says Greenman.
'We're having a summer party,' says Nico.
'And what's the matter?'
'Fox has got the food!' says Sam.
'Oh, no!'
'I'm hungry and thirsty,' says Nico.

'I'm hungry and thirsty, too,' says Sam.
'I've got an idea!' says Greenman.
'Yummy!' says Fox.
'Food for me!'

'Hello, Greenman,' says Hen.
'Hello, Hen. Have you got any eggs?'
'Yes, I have.'
'Can I have some eggs, please?'
'Yes. I like sharing my eggs. Here you are.'
'Thank you!'
'One, two, three, four, five, six.'

'Hello, Greenman.' says Rabbit.
'Hello, Rabbit. Have you got any carrots?'
'Yes, I have.'
'Can I have some carrots, please?'
'Yes. I like sharing my carrots. Here you are.'
'Thank you!'
'One, two, three, four, five, six.'

'Hello, Greenman,' says Tree.
'Hello, Tree. Have you got any plums?'
'Yes, I have.'
'Can I have some plums, please?'
'Yes. I like sharing my plums. Here you are.'
'Thank you!'
'One, two, three, four, five, six.'

'Hello, Fox!'
'Hello, Greenman. I'm sorry. I'm sad on my own.
Can I share my food, too?'
'Yes. We like sharing. Here you are.'

'Welcome to the summer party!' says Sam.
'Thank you for the food,' says Nico.
'I like sharing my eggs,' says Hen.
'I like sharing my carrots,' says Rabbit.
'I like sharing my plums,' says Tree.
'I like sharing my food, too,' says Fox.
'I'm hungry and thirsty. Let's eat! Happy summer,
everyone!' says Greenman.

🍃 Table time

Say the Table time chant (see page 11).

📑 Pupil's Book page 75. Worksheet 2. Look, match and say.

Show pupils page 75 and walk around to check that everyone is on the correct page. Point to the picture of Hen and say *What has Hen got in the story?* Hold up different flashcards to show food items. *Has she got potatoes? No. Has she got carrots? No. Has she got eggs? Yes! Let's draw a line to the eggs.* Show in your own book how to draw a line from Hen to the eggs. Repeat the process with Rabbit's carrots, and Tree's plums. Say *(Hen) says 'I like sharing my (eggs). Here you are.'*

🍃 Goodbye

Follow the description on page 9.

🍃 Extra activities

📑 Pupil's Book page 76. Extra activity: Trace and colour the picture.

Say *Look, a picnic basket. Let's trace the lines.* Show pupils how to trace the lines of the basket. Then, say *Where's the carrot?* Point to the carrot in your own book. Check that pupils are pointing to the correct item. Repeat with the other food items, then say *Now colour the picture.* Monitor as pupils work asking questions to individual pupils, such as *What colour is the egg?*

Teacher Resources Worksheet 25: Make a food wheel.

Pass out the worksheets or ask your helper. Hold up a prepared example, with the arrow held in the centre of the food wheel with a paper fastener. Spin the wheel and ask Greenman *Can I have some (carrots)?* Greenman says *Yes. Here you are.* and pretends to give you the carrots. Repeat with two other items. Say *Now let's make your wheel!* Pass out scissors and be prepared to attach the arrow with a paper fastener to each circle. When pupils have finished, they can practise spinning the wheel and asking each other for the food.

✏️ Activity Book page 35 – Find and make

Pupils find natural materials and use them to make a bird's nest. Pupils can find the natural materials outside or you can bring the materials to class for pupils to find. Pupils will need twigs, leaves, moss or grass, flowers and big round or egg-shaped stones.

Use the individual pictures in the book to talk about the different natural materials. Point to the nest in the book and tell pupils they are going to make a nest with the natural materials.

Pupils look for the natural materials, either outside or among the materials that have been brought to the classroom. Encourage them to look for round/oval stones for the eggs. When they find an item, they circle it in their book.

☺ **Now you!** Pupils work in pairs to make a nest with the materials. They can imagine making it for their favourite bird.

🙆 **I can do it.** Praise pupils for making the nests and remind them of how many things they can do. Pupils repeat the affirmation *I can do it* with you.

🌱 Help pupils learn about birds and their habitats. Teach them how birds create their nests to be secure and keep warm and comfortable (they use moss for the padding and lining), and how they keep their eggs warm so they will hatch.

Lesson ③

Lesson objective
To introduce a contrasting concept (hungry/thirsty), and a value (sharing).

Language
New: *hungry/thirsty; Have you got any (eggs)? Here you are.* food
Review: *Yes, I have. good/naughty, up/down, clean/dirty, big/small, strong/weak;* colours; numbers 1–6
Receptive: *Let's stick. Let's put our string on. Show me your (blue) crayon. Let's circle the things for (thirsty).*

Materials
Presentation Plus, Big Book story Unit 6, PB page 77, Flashcards Unit 6, Pop-out Unit 6, glue sticks, 1 piece of string per pupil, Class Audio, plasticine or plastic food, homemade flashcards showing *good/naughty, up/down, clean/dirty, big/small, strong/weak, hungry/thirsty,* crayons, pencils. Optional: PB page 78, Teacher Resources Worksheet 26, AB page 36

 Use Presentation Plus to do the activity.

Name _____

77

🖜 Starting the lesson

Settle the class with an opening routine (see Teacher's Book pages 8 and 9).

🖜 Active time

Warmer

Review the Unit 6 Flashcards by playing the *Remember the cards* game (follow the description on page 19).

Do a role-play.

Use realia or plasticine food from the previous lesson. Put the food on a tray or in a box. Choose a volunteer to help. Say *I'm hungry. Have you got any (eggs)?* **Help the pupil to say** *Yes, I have. Here you are.* **Say** *Thank you.* Practise the dialogue with various pupils, changing between *hungry* and *thirsty* and asking for different items. Then call a pupil up to say your role, helping with the lines and whispering them for the pupils to repeat, as necessary.

Do a concepts review.

Review the contrasting concepts from previous units, with actions, and practise the new concept *hungry/thirsty.* Before the lesson, prepare homemade flashcards with pictures showing the contrasting concepts. Have pupils sit in a circle, and place the flashcards face down in the centre. Model how to select one and act it out. Motion for the pupils to guess the word. Say the word for them to repeat, if necessary. Call a volunteer to take one card and act it out. The other pupils guess the word. Repeat until most or all of the pupils have had a turn.

Good/naughty (Thumbs up/thumbs down.)

Up/down (Raise your hands up high over your head/squat down and touch your toes.)

Clean/dirty (Pretend to 'wash' your hands and then smile/look at your hands and then scrunch your nose and look away.)

Big/small (Stretch your arms wide at your sides/hold the index finger and thumb of each hand together to make a very small shape in front of you.)

Strong/weak (Make muscles with your arms/let your arms hang at your sides and hunch your shoulders over.)

Hungry/thirsty (Rub your tummy/hold your throat and hang out your tongue as if parched.)

🖜 Story time

Say the Story time chant *It's story time, story time, open the Big Book and look inside* and motion opening a book. Take out the Big Book to show the parts of the story where we can see people that are hungry or thirsty. Say *Who's hungry and thirsty? (Nico and Sam.) Who's got all the food? (Fox.) What has Fox got? (A banana and sausages.)* Be sure to use actions for *hungry* and *thirsty* and the food items, to make the message clear.

Reread the story or listen to the audio (Track 53).

▷ You may also choose to use the story video, pausing the video rather than pointing to pictures.

🍃 Table time

Say the Table time chant (see page 11).

Do the pop-out activity.

Direct pupils' attention to the sample pop-out you have prepared: a party hat. Say *It's a party. Let's make our party hats!*

Show pupils how to take out the pop-out carefully. Give pupils time to colour the balloons on their hats. When all the pupils have finished, say *Let's stick our hats together.* Pass out glue sticks. Model how to roll the pop-out into a hat shape and glue the two ends together. Have pupils hold up their hats to show you once they have finished. Then give each pupil a piece of string (with a knot on one end). Say *Now, let's put our string on our party hats.* Model how to thread the string through one of the holes in the party hat. (You will need to show that the knot holds the string onto the hat.) Then help pupils to thread the string through the second hole and tie another knot to hold it onto the hat (you may need to do this yourself). Say *Now, let's wear our party hats!*

Let pupils wear their party hats while they listen to the story again.

📖 **Pupil's Book page 77. Worksheet 3: Say *hungry* or *thirsty* and circle.**

Show pupils page 77 and walk around to check that everyone is on the correct page. Say *Point to Sam. Is she hungry or thirsty?* Elicit the response *Thirsty.* Say *Good! Point to Nico. Is he hungry or thirsty?* Elicit the response *Hungry.* Say *Well done. Show me your blue crayon.* Hold up your blue crayon. *Excellent. Let's circle the things for thirsty Sam* (do a gesture for thirsty) *in blue.* Show them how to do this in your book. When pupils have finished circling the water and juice, repeat the process for Nico with *hungry*, circling the food items in red.

🍃 Goodbye

Follow the description on page 9.

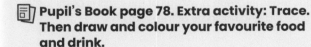

🍃 Extra activities

📖 **Pupil's Book page 78. Extra activity: Trace. Then draw and colour your favourite food and drink.**

Have pupils open their books to page 78. Say *Let's trace the lines.* Model how to trace the lines of the glass and plate.

Show the *plum* flashcard. Say *I like to eat plums* and do a 'thumbs up' and smile. Shrug your shoulders and point to the pupils as you say *What do you like, (Mario)?* Help the pupil to say a food. Ask several pupils the same question. Then say *Draw what you like.* Act as if you are drawing a picture on the plate in your book. Then repeat this process for *drink*, saying *I like to drink juice. What do you like, (Lucía)?*

Walk around the class to monitor and be sure everyone has understood. Give pupils time to colour their pictures. You may choose to have them share their pictures with the class. Help with vocabulary, as necessary.

Value activity: Sharing

In Lesson 2, the pupils say *I like sharing* as part of a dialogue and they have heard the phrase in the Unit 6 story, so it should be familiar. Point out the parts of the story in the Big Book where we see animals sharing. Point out Fox in the story who doesn't share, but later says *'I'm sorry'* and does share. Model a situation in which a person doesn't want to share. Hold something close to you as if to hide it and say *I don't want to share! It's mine!* Then look at all the pupils and say *Oh, I'm sorry. I can share.* Model how the pupils can say *Hooray!* Have various pupils act this out. You can whisper words in their ear to repeat, or have them act out the situation without words

Emotions: Being sorry

In L1, talk about why Fox is sorry in the story *(he's upset his friends, he's by himself)* and how he feels *(sad).* Ask *How does he feel when he shares the food? (Happy!)*

📖 **Teacher Resources Worksheet 26: Look and circle.**

Pass out the worksheets, or ask your helper. Say *Look at the boy in the picture. What's the matter? Yes, he's thirsty. What can they share?* Help pupils to find the picture with the boy sharing his juice. Say *Circle sharing the juice.* Repeat the process with the hungry girl.

📖 Activity Book page 36 – Feel

Review food words. Use photos of a campfire cook out and ask pupils to guess what food the people might be cooking. Elicit ideas including *sausages*.

Pupils look at the maze activity in the book. Point to the empty frying pan in the centre of the maze and ask if there's any food. *(No.)* Then point to the person cooking and elicit how he feels. *(Hungry.)* Finally point to the child at the start of the maze and ask how he can help. *(He can bring food.)*

Pupils draw a line through the maze to reach the pan, colouring the sausages along the way. Count the sausages together and draw them in the pan.

🙌 **I am helpful.** Remind pupils that the child in the book, collects sausages to help the adult make a meal for them both. Ask pupils how they are helpful (at home and in class). Pupils then repeat the affirmation *I am helpful* with you.

🙂 **Now you!** Arrange a cook out in the playground or another open space. Alternatively, have a pretend cook out in the classroom with a 'fire' made from sticks and red and orange tissue paper, and sausages made of plasticine.

🌱 Make sure pupils understand the rules of cooking outside. They should put a slab on the ground to protect the grass or other undergrowth. Fires should never be left unattended and should always be put out completely at the end.

Lesson 4

Lesson objective
To use TPR to review unit vocabulary through an action song.

Language
New: *Let's have a picnic. I am (hungry/thirsty). Let's eat (carrots). Let's drink juice.* food
Review: weather; colours; numbers 1–6
Receptive: *What's missing? Let's count the (eggs). Circle the (eggs). Look for more differences.*

Materials
Presentation Plus, PB page 79, Flashcards Unit 6, Class Audio, crayons, pencils. Optional: PB page 80, real or plasticine/plastic foods, box or bag, blindfold/sleep mask, AB page 37

 Use Presentation Plus to watch the action song video. ▷

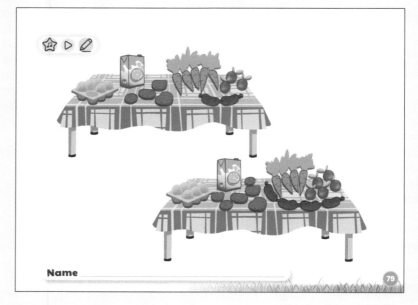

Name _____ 79

🍃 Starting the lesson

Settle the class with an opening routine (see Teacher's Book pages 8 and 9).

🍃 Active time

Warmer

Review the Unit 6 Flashcards by holding each one up and eliciting the vocabulary word from the class. Then, hold up two or three at a time and say the word for one of the cards you are holding. Choose a volunteer to go to the front and point to the correct word. Say *I'm hungry!* Exaggerate holding your tummy and make a rumbling tummy noise. Have pupils copy you, or give them turns to show how they can act very hungry.

Say *Guess, am I hungry or thirsty?* Do the action for *hungry*. Elicit the response. Call on volunteers to act out *hungry* and *thirsty* for the class to guess.

Game: *What's missing?*

Place the Unit 6 Flashcards face up on the floor. Say *There are six cards. Now close your eyes.* Use gestures and model how to do this by covering your eyes with your hands. Take one card away from the group of six. Say *Open your eyes. One, two, three, four, five cards! What's missing?* If the pupils have trouble understanding the concept, hold up the flashcard that you have taken out of the group, facing away from them. Say *What's this?* Help pupils by naming the other cards. When the pupils guess the secret card, repeat the process by taking away a different flashcard. A volunteer could also play the teacher's part in this game.

Let's have a picnic action song: Watch the video. Sing and do the actions.

▷ You may prefer to use the action song video to teach the pupils the actions and the song.

First, play the audio and hold up flashcards for the vocabulary words in the song. Invite the pupils to say the food when you hold up the card. The second time you play the song, do the actions to show the class. Next, have the pupils stand up *(Stand up, stand up, 1-2-3. Stand up, stand up tall with me.)* Teach them the actions as you say each line of the song.

Practise the actions for the song three or four times slowly, going through the song line by line. Then, play the audio track and do the actions together. Repeat until all of the class is participating in each action and singing some of the words.

 ### 54 Let's have a picnic

It's a hot day, it's a sunny day. (Fan yourself, shade your eyes with your hand.)

I am thirsty, I am hungry.
(Hold your throat and let your tongue hang out as if parched, rub your tummy.)

It's a hot day, it's a sunny day. (Do action as above.)

Let's have a picnic with our friends!
(Spread your hands out as if indicating the tablecloth, motion for people to come near.)

Let's have a picnic with our friends. (Do action as above.)

Let's have a picnic, we can share. (Spread out a tablecloth, hold one hand like a plate and pass out imaginary items from the plate.)

Let's have a picnic with our friends. (Do action as above.)

I am thirsty and hungry! (Do action as above.)

1 Carrots, carrots. Let's eat carrots! (Hold an imaginary carrot in your hand and pretend to take a big bite.)

2 Potatoes, potatoes. Let's eat potatoes! (Hold up two fingers, put your fingers together to make a round shape like a potato)

3 Eggs, eggs. Let's eat eggs! (Hold up three fingers, put your thumb and one finger together to make an oval shape, like an egg.)

4 Sausages, sausages. Let's eat sausages! (Hold up four fingers, pretend to pull out a chain of sausage links out of your opposite hand.)

5 Plums, plums. Let's eat plums! (Hold up five fingers, pretend to take a bite out of a juicy plum.)

6 Juice, juice. Let's drink juice! (Hold up six fingers, pretend to pour juice into a glass and then drink it.)

🌢 Table time

Say the Table time chant (see page 11).

📖 Pupil's Book page 79. Worksheet 4: Find and circle the five differences.

Show pupils page 79 and walk around to check that everyone is on the correct page. Point to the two pictures in your book for the class to see. Say *Look for the differences. Look at the eggs in this picture.* (point) *Let's count the eggs: one, two, three, four, five. Now look at the eggs in this picture.* (point) *Let's count the eggs: one, two, three, four, five, six! Circle the eggs, they are different!* Model circling the eggs with your finger.

Say *Now look for four more differences!* Monitor pupils as they work and offer help. When the pupils have finished, use the same process to review the answers.

🌢 Goodbye

Follow the description on page 9.

🌢 Extra activities

📖 Pupil's Book page 80. Extra activity: Draw and colour yourself and your friends.

Say *Look! A picnic! The picnic needs people! I'm going to draw me and my friends having a picnic. Here is one friend, Mary.* (Draw a simple picture.) *Here is my friend, James* (draw a simple picture) *and here is me!* (Draw a simple picture.) *Now, you draw!*

As you monitor, ask pupils about their friends' clothes and the colours they are using. You may choose to have them share their pictures with the class when they have finished.

Game: *Touch and guess*

The pupils guess a food (real, plastic or plasticine) by touching it, with their eyes covered. First introduce each food item for the pupils to identify. Say *Look what we have! What's this?* Name each food.

Choose a volunteer and cover his/her eyes. Take out some food from a box or bag and hand it to the volunteer. Let the other pupils see. Ask *What is it, (Mario)? Is it a (potato)?* Say an incorrect food so that the pupil can guess. Help him/her if necessary. Applaud the pupil for participating. Continue the process until each pupil who wants to participate has had a turn. (Some pupils may prefer not to participate. They will still learn from the activity and practise vocabulary.)

📝 Activity Book page 37 – Investigate

Review foods and introduce the concept of food that comes from plants or animals. Use images in the Unit 6 Big Book story to elicit the foods that come from plants (*carrots, potatoes and plums*) and food that comes from an animal (*the eggs from the hen*).

Direct pupils' attention to the pictures of milk, carrots, eggs and apple juice in the book and have pupils guess where the different food comes from. Pupils can finger trace the lines to check their answers, then trace over the lines with pencil. You could ask pupils which of the foods come from plants/animals.

☺ **Now you!** Encourage pupils to think about other food they like to eat, and find out where it comes from.

🙆 **I am interested in things.** Praise pupils for finding out where some of the food they eat comes from. Remind pupils that it's good to be curious about the world around them so they can learn about it. Encourage pupils to repeat the affirmation *I am interested in things* with you.

🌱 Help pupils appreciate our connection to nature by teaching them where the food we eat and drink comes from.

Lesson 5

Lesson objective
To work on pre-writing skills and practise numbers through a song.

Language
New: *tomato;* food
Review: *Here you are.* shapes; colours; numbers *1–6*
Receptive: *Let's count the (potatoes). Let's draw a line. Let's trace the numbers.*

Materials
Presentation Plus, Big Book story Unit 6, PB page 81, Class Audio, groups of 6 classroom objects, crayons, pencils. Optional: PB page 82, plasticine, Teacher Resources Worksheet 27, AB page 38

 Use Presentation Plus to do the activities.

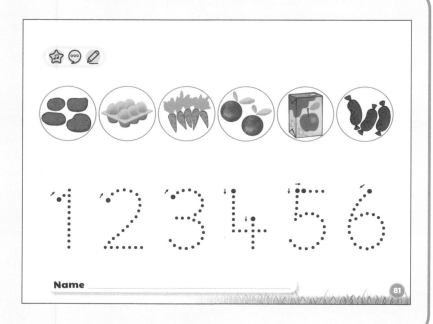

Name

81

Starting the lesson

Settle the class with an opening routine (see Teacher's Book pages 8 and 9).

Active time

Warmer

Review shapes, colours and numbers (you can use the Routine Boards or Flashcards on Presentation Plus for this).

Game: *Find the number*

Play this game with six classroom objects. Follow the procedure on page 18.

Six tomatoes number song 1–6: Sing and count.

Say *We know our numbers very well! Let's practise a song with them.* Show pupils a picture of some tomatoes and say that they are going to sing a song about tomatoes. Have the pupils sit or stand and tell them to listen for numbers. Play the song holding up your fingers for the numbers. Next, say the song line by line doing the actions. Do this three times. Then play the audio again. Repeat until the pupils are singing many of the words, focusing on the number words.

---

55 Six tomatoes

*How many **tomatoes** can you see?* (Make a questioning gesture, point below your eye.)

*I can see 6 **tomatoes**.*
(Point below your eye, hold up six fingers.)

Count with me!
(Motion as if including someone in a group.)

*1 **red tomato**.* (Hold up one finger.)

*2 **red tomatoes**.* (Hold up two fingers.)

*3 **red tomatoes**.* (Hold up three fingers.)

*4 **red tomatoes**.* (Hold up four fingers.)

*5 **red tomatoes**.* (Hold up five fingers.)

*6 **red tomatoes**!* (Hold up six fingers.)

Repeat with:
orange carrot(s), brown sausage(s), purple plum(s), yellow egg(s)

🖋 Table time

Say the Table time chant (see page 11).

📖 Pupil's Book page 81. Worksheet 5: Count, match and trace.

Show pupils page 81 and walk around to check that everyone is on the correct page. Hold up your own book and point out the different foods. Say *Let's count the potatoes.* Choose the circle with four potatoes. Say *One, two, three, four! Four potatoes! Let's draw a line to the number 4!* Show how to draw a line from the picture up to the number 4. Continue with other examples, or let the pupils finish on their own as you monitor.

When they have finished, say *Let's trace the numbers 1–6.* Show in your book how to trace the numbers. The pupils should be familiar with the process. Monitor as they work. Review the answers together as a class.

🖋 Goodbye

Follow the description on page 9.

🖋 Extra activities

📖 Pupil's Book page 82. Extra activity: Trace. Then draw six eggs.

Show pupils page 82 and walk around to check that everyone is on the correct page. Say *Look, it's Rabbit. Rabbit has got a basket. Let's trace the lines on the basket.* Model how to trace the lines in your book. Then say *Rabbit is hungry. He looks for …* Hold up the egg flashcard to elicit the answer *eggs.* Say *Yes, eggs. How many eggs?* Count on your fingers one to six. Say *Six eggs. Let's draw six eggs in Rabbit's basket.* Model drawing the eggs in your own book. Then, say *What colour are eggs?* The pupils will probably say, white or brown, but you could tell them that some hens lay eggs that are blue or pink, too! Allow the pupils to colour. When they have finished, say *Point and count, one, two, three, four, five, six. Six eggs, well done!*

Make plasticine numbers.

The pupils use plasticine to make numbers. Before passing out plasticine to the class, make an example in front of them. Make a number 1. Say *Number 1. Repeat, number 1.* Make a number 2. Say *Number 2, repeat, number 2. Let's make numbers!*

Prepare to pass out a ball of plasticine to each pupil and say *One, two, three hands on your knees.* Model to show that children should keep their hands on their knees until they have permission to begin. When everyone has plasticine, look around and say *Look. Ready? Go. Make number 4.* Say this in a calm voice so that they know there's no need to rush. When all the pupils have finished, have them hold up their numbers and repeat them after you. Monitor the pupils as they work and help those who struggle.

Teacher Resources Worksheet 27: Listen and colour. Then colour by number.

Pass out the worksheets, or ask your helper. Tell pupils to prepare their crayons. Say *Colour 1 red* (show them how to colour in the number 1 spot in the colour key), *colour 2 orange, colour 3 brown, colour 4 purple, colour 5 yellow and colour 6 green.* Pause and repeat throughout. When you have checked that all the pupils have the colour key completed correctly, point to the number 1 circle and say *OK, this is 1, it is red. Let's colour.* Pupils find 1 in the picture and identify the food (tomatoes). Say *Colour the tomatoes red.* Repeat this process until children are able to continue on their own. Encourage pupils to say the numbers and colours.

📖 Activity Book page 38 – Practise

Review food vocabulary and numbers 1–6. Then talk about the food from the unit. Decide which food comes from a plant, and whether it grows in the ground or on a tree.

Direct pupils' attention to the pictures of carrots in the book. First, count the carrots in the ground and those that have just been picked (count them separately and then all together). Then count the carrots on the plate and have pupils notice that it is the same number. Have pupils trace the numbers next to the pictures, then repeat the process with the potatoes and plums.

🙌 **I am clever.** Congratulate pupils for how well they know their numbers 1–6 in English, and how they can count different groups of items and add them together. Pupils repeat the affirmation *I am clever* with you.

🙂 **Now you!** Pupils can plant seeds to start a growing project, e.g. they can plant cress seeds in egg shells to grow cress heads.

🌱 Help pupils understand what plants need to grow, and learn about the food we get from plants.

Lesson 6

Lesson objective
To consolidate all unit content.

Language
Review: food; Big Book language structures
Receptive: *Your turn. Choose a card.*
Find and stick.

Materials
Presentation Plus, Greenman Puppet, PB page 83, Flashcards Unit 6, Class Audio, Stickers Unit 6, soft ball, crayons, pencils. Optional: AB page 39

 Use Presentation Plus to play the games.

Consolidation — WORKSHEET 6

Find, stick and say.

Name

83

Starting the lesson

Settle the class with an opening routine (see Teacher's Book pages 8 and 9)

Active time

Warmer

Review flashcards from the unit by spreading various cards face down in the centre of the circle. Model the activity yourself first. Turn over a card and say the word. Choose a pupil. Say *(Lucía), your turn. Choose a card.* Help the pupil to say the word if necessary. Give several pupils a turn. You may wish to use the audio of the unit vocabulary to review (Track 51).

Game: *Roll and review*

Follow the description on page 19.

Story review

Say the Story time chant (see page 10) and motion opening a book. Reread the story, inviting the pupils to participate in saying the words or lines that they know.

▷ Alternatively, you may want to play the story video.

Table time

Say the Table time chant (see page 11).

 Pupil's Book page 83. Worksheet 6: Find, stick and say.

Help the pupils to find page 83 in the Pupil's Book and locate the stickers for Unit 6. Say *Find and stick the pictures.* Have Greenman repeat each word several times, as pupils look for the correct sticker to put in each place. Monitor the children as they work and encourage them along, or give gesture clues. Repeat with each vocabulary word. When they have finished, have pupils point to each sticker and say the word.

Goodbye

Follow the description on page 9.

Activity Book page 39 – Care

Review the word *juice* and any fruits that pupils know. Ask pupils what kind of juice they like.

Direct pupils' attention to the picture of the juice-making machine in the book. Elicit what fruits are already going into the juice machine (apples and plums), and encourage them to suggest other fruits that they like and want to add. Pupils can use L1, but translate the fruit names into English. Pupils then draw their chosen fruits into the feed lines of the juice machine.

Pupils then think what colour each fruit's juice would be and colour the juice in the machine.

I share with my friends. Congratulate pupils for completing the activity in the book so that the friends can share the juice together. In L1, ask pupils why it's important to be kind and share things with your friends, and talk about the things they share. Pupils repeat the affirmation *I share with my friends* with you.

Now you! Bring a smoothie machine or blender and some fruit into class so that pupils can pick their own fruit juice combinations to try out. Remember to always check for allergies with parents before tasting food or drink in class.

Teach pupils about different kinds of fruits and the purpose of them. Explain that fruits contain the seeds needed to grow new plants.

To end the unit, pupils circle the fox on page 3.

Extra Phonics Lesson

Lesson objective
To introduce two new phonics sounds ('x' and 'ng')

Language
New: *fox, box, wing, sing*

Materials
Presentation Plus, PB page 84, downloadable Phonics Flashcards, Class Audio, crayons, pencils. Optional: Teacher Resources Worksheet 28, scissors, glue sticks

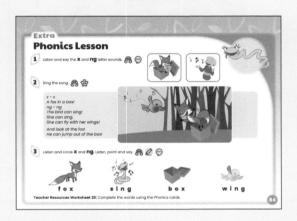

🔖 Phonics time

Warmer

Show pupils the *x* and *ng* Phonics Flashcards. Read the words, then segment the sounds. Say *Look at the picture: There is a fox. Listen to the sound: x. Listen and repeat: fo-x-x-x-x.* Repeat with the second sound. Point to the the Phonics Flashcards and say the sounds three times, asking different pupils to repeat after you.

Pupil's Book page 84. 1. Listen and say the *x* and *ng* letter sounds.

Say *Point to the 'fox' picture. Point to the 'sing' picture. Say x-x-x, ng-ng-ng.* Point to the correct picture in your own book to give clues. Repeat the words in different orders and monitor to check pupils are pointing to the right pictures. Play the audio and have pupils listen and repeat the sounds and words. Repeat three times.

> 🎧 **56**
> x – x – x   fox   box   fox in a box
> ng – ng – ng   sing

Pupil's Book page 84. 2. Sing the song.

Show pupils the picture in activity 2. Play the song. Point to items in the picture to help pupils understand meaning. After playing the track three times, say it slowly and have pupils repeat each line, while looking at the picture. Play the audio again. Continue repeating it until pupils can say at least the *fox, box* and *sing* parts of the song.

> 🎧 **57**
> x – x
> A fox in a box!
> ng – ng
> The bird can sing!
> She can sing.
> She can fly with her wings!
> And look at the fox!
> He can jump out of the box!

Pupil's Book page 84. 3. Listen and circle *x* and *ng*. Listen, point and say.

Show pupils activity 3 in your book. Point to the first picture and say the word *fox*. Say *Let's listen.* Play the first part of the audio and point to each picture as the word is said in the audio. After listening once, say *Let's circle the 'x' sound.* Play the audio again and model how to circle the *x*. Give hints by smiling or nodding when the word has the *x* sound and shaking your head when it doesn't. Review the correct answers together. Then repeat the process with the *ng* sound. You could have pupils circle the two sounds in different colours. Pupils then listen to the second part of the audio and point and say the words.

> 🎧 **58**
> fox   sing   box   wing
> sing   box   wing   fox

🔖 Extra activities

Teacher Resources Worksheet 28: Complete the words using the Phonics cards.

Prepare the worksheets for the class in advance. Say *Let's cut out our Phonics cards.* Model how to cut out the letter cards, then have pupils lay them out on the table. Say *Listen to the words and put the 'x' sound or the 'ng' sound in its place.* Say each word slowly (*fox, sing, box,* and *wing*) emphasising the final consonant letter sound. Encourage pupils to repeat the words as they stick the letters in their place. When they have finished matching, they can colour the pictures.

Review 3

Spring fun!

Lesson objective

To review vocabulary from Units 5 and 6 and sing a song about spring.

Language

Review: *green, pink; flower; rainy, sunny, windy; farm animals and food*
Receptive: *Let's grow up like a flower. Point to the (farm). Where does the (carrot) go?*

Materials

Presentation Plus, Greenman Puppet, PB page 85, Flashcards Units 5 and 6, Class Audio, flowers (real or artificial), crayons, pencils. Optional: PB page 86, Teacher Resources Worksheets 29 and 30, paints, scissors, glue sticks, a piece of string per pupil

🖙 Starting the lesson

Settle the class with an opening routine (see Teacher's Book pages 8 and 9).

🖙 Active time

Warmer

Review weather vocabulary (you could use the Routine Boards on Presentation Plus to do this). Pupils can choose the vocabulary that is most appropriate for spring. Have the pupils use gestures to show the different types of weather. (Show rain falling with your fingers, blow out air and move your hands in swirling motions for *windy*, and make a big sun over your head with your arms for *sunny*.) Ask *What's the weather like today? Is it sunny? Is it cold? Is it rainy? Is it spring?*

Say the vocabulary.

Have Greenman hold up each of the Flashcards from Units 5 and 6. Have the pupils say (or repeat) each word. Then, speed up to get the children to identify the words as quickly as possible.

Spring is here! song: Sing and do the actions.

Show the pupils the flowers that you have brought to class. Hold one up and say *What colour is the flower?* Elicit vocabulary for the green of the stem and the appropriate colour for the petals. Say *Let's grow up like a flower!* Show them how the flower grows up from the soil by using your hand or cover the flower with a book and slowly reveal it. Model how to do this with your body for the pupils to copy. As you grow say *The flower grows up, up, up, up … Spring is here!* Practise this two or three times.

Play the song once and model the actions. Then, have the pupils join in as you say the song line by line and do the actions with them. Repeat this until most pupils are saying some of the words and participating in the actions. Then play the song again, modelling the actions with the pupils participating. Repeat the song until the class is singing most of the words and doing the actions.

 Spring is here!

Spring-a-ling-a-ling-a-ling-a-ling-a-ling-a-ling. (Wiggle your hips.)

Spring is here! (Stretch your hands up and out as if making a big announcement.)

The sun comes up to say hello. (Put your arms in front of you, elbows bent, resting one forearm on top of the other, lift up your right hand like a rising sun and then wave hello.)

Green and pink the flowers grow. (Dip your hands down in front of you, then raise your palms up like two growing flowers.)

Spring is here! (Stretch your hands up and out as if making a big announcement.)

The happy forest sings a song. (Move your fingers as if you are conducting an orchestra.)

Frogs and rabbits jump along. (Jump in place.)

Spring is here! (Stretch your hands up and out as if making a big announcement.)

The happy birds sing a song. (Move your fingers like you are conducting an orchestra.)

Baby animals sing along. (Cradle an imaginary baby in your arms.)

Spring is here! (Stretch your hands up and out as if making a big announcement.)

🍃 Table time

Say the Table Time chant (see page 11).

📖 Pupil's Book page 85. Worksheet 1: Look, match and say.

Show pupils page 85 and walk around to check that everyone is on the correct page. Look at the photos of the farm and picnic together and elicit what pupils can see in each one. Say each of the vocabulary words: *horse, cow, sheep, hen, pig, rabbit, egg, potato, carrot, sausage, plum, juice*, and have pupils point to the correct pictures. Now say *Point to the farm … Point to the picnic. Where do the animals live?* (Pupils point to the photo of the farm.) *Where is the food?* (Pupils point to the photo of the picnic.) Then ask *Where does the carrot go?* Model how to draw a line from the carrot to the photo of the picnic. Pupils should be able to finish this independently as you monitor their work. Review answers as a class by asking *What's on the farm/in the picnic?* Pupils say the correct answers together.

🍃 Goodbye

Follow the description on page 9.

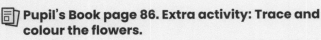
🍃 Extra activities

📖 Pupil's Book page 86. Extra activity: Trace and colour the flowers.

Show one of the flowers that you have brought to class and trace the lines around it gently with your finger. Say *Look at the shape of the flower. Draw a flower in the air.* Model how to do this. If you have brought different types of flowers, encourage pupils to notice how the petals are different colours and shapes. Now, hold up your book to show how to trace the lines of the flowers in the book. Say *Let's trace the lines and colour.* Pupils should be able to work independently on this. Monitor as they work.

Game: *Point to the word*

Place Flashcards from Units 5 and 6 on the walls around the classroom. Say/Sing the *Farm animal* rap (Track 44) and the *Have you got an egg, please?* song (Track 52) while playing this game. Follow the description on page 18.

Teacher Resources Worksheets 29 and 30: Paint, cut and stick to make a spring string.

Make sure each pupil has the spring project worksheets and a piece of string (half a metre long). Prepare an example of a completed spring project to show the class. Play the song *Spring is here!* (Track 59) again. Say *Let's make a spring string.* Hold up your example and say *Point to the flowers.* (point to a flower on your string) *Here are the flowers!* Have the pupils point to the flowers on Worksheet 29. Say *Point to the sun. Here is the sun.* Have the pupils repeat the procedure for the rabbits and frogs on Worksheet 30. Say *Now let's paint!* Give the pupils time to paint the different spring pictures. When they have finished, say *Now let's cut out the flowers, the sun, the rabbits and the frogs and put them on our string!* Monitor as the pupils cut out the pictures along the dotted lines. Say *Now let's put our spring things on the string!* Model sticking each cut-out picture to the string (alternatively, you may wish to make holes in the pictures so that the pupils can thread the string through the holes). If the pupils find this difficult, they can leave their pictures for you to attach to the string later. Make a spring display with the spring strings.

World Peace Day

Lesson objective

To introduce vocabulary related to World Peace Day and a new phonics sound ('w').

Language

New: *dove, peace, world*
Review: *children, friends; colours; numbers 1–6*
Receptive: *Let's (listen). Show me. Point.*

Materials

Presentation Plus, PB pages 87 and 88, World Peace Day Flashcards and downloadable Phonics Flashcards, World Peace Day Pop-outs, Class Audio, crayons, pencils. Optional: Teacher Resources Worksheets 31 and 32, scissors, glue sticks

Teacher Resources Worksheet 31: Draw and colour. Then cut out and stick.

Name _____

dove, peace, world 87

🔖 Starting the lesson

Settle the class with an opening routine (see Teacher's Book pages 8 and 9).

🔖 Active time

Warmer

Say *Today is World Peace Day. We are friends with everyone and we are happy!* Review the colour *white* and teach vocabulary for World Peace Day with the World Peace Day Flashcards: *world, peace* and *dove*. At this point, you may wish to use the audio of the vocabulary to listen and repeat as a class.

 dove, peace, world

🔖 Table time

Say the Table time chant (see page 11).

Pupil's Book page 87. Worksheet 1: Listen, point and say. Then colour.

Help pupils to find the correct page. Hold up your book and point to the different World Peace Day vocabulary words in the picture (for *peace* you can point to the children holding hands). Say the vocabulary for pupils to repeat after you *world, dove, peace.* Have them count the children in the picture.

Say *Let's listen!* Play the dialogue once. The children listen and point to the vocabulary items as they hear them. Then play it again, line by line, and have the children repeat each line. Do this until most of the class is participating and saying many of the words. Then play the dialogue several more times, stopping it at various points for children to say the next word.

Direct pupils' attention to the uncoloured pictures. Say *Let's colour the world blue and green.* Demonstrate how to colour the sea blue and the land green. Point to the dove and say *What colour?* Yes, white. Point out, or elicit, that pupils don't have to colour the dove as it is already white! Let pupils colour the children however they wish, so that they are unique.

Boy:	*Ooh, look! It's the world.*
Girl:	*Oh, yes. The world.*
Boy:	*And look at the dove! It's white.*
Girl:	*Yes, it's a white dove. It's World Peace Day!*
Boy:	*And children! Look at the children!*
Girl:	*Yes. The children are different, but they're friends.*
Boy:	*Yes. They're friends and they're happy.*
Girl:	*The children are happy and the dove is white. It's World Peace Day!*
Both:	*It's World Peace Day! Hooray!*

Do the pop-out activity.

Direct pupils' attention to the sample pop-out that you have prepared: a 3D dove. Hold up the dove and say *Look at the dove! It's World Peace Day.* Remind children that the dove is the symbol for peace.

Show pupils how to take out the pop-out pieces carefully (popping out the slit in the body for the wings as well). Then show them how to put the wings through the slit to make the dove. Observe as they do this and help as needed.

When all the pupils have finished, say *Show me your dove.* Model holding up your dove by its body, and moving it gently up and down in the air, making it 'fly'. Say *Let's listen.* Play the dialogue (Track 61). Pupils listen to the dialogue, and hold their doves up when they hear the word *dove.* When they hear *It's World Peace Day!,* they make their doves fly in a circle above their heads.

Pupils can take their dove pop-outs home, or you may wish to hang them in the classroom as part of a World Peace Day display.

Extra Phonics Lesson

🔊 Phonics time

📖 Pupil's Book page 88. 1. Listen and say the *w* letter sound.

Review previous phonics sounds using the Phonics Flashcards. Review *world* with the World Peace Day Phonics Flashcard. Point to the picture for the sound in your book and repeat the sound as you point *w-w-world.* Play the audio and have pupils listen and repeat three times.

 62 *w – w – w   world*

📖 Pupil's Book page 88. 2. Sing the song.

Play the song. Point to the picture to help pupils understand meaning. Play it again and introduce some actions. After playing the track three times, say it slowly, line by line, and have pupils repeat each line (following your lead to use gestures where possible). Play the song again and repeat until pupils are singing at least the *This is our world, Our wonderful world* parts of the song, and are showing comprehension through gestures.

 63
w – w – w world
This is our world, (Draw a large circle in front of you with both hands.)
Our wonderful world. (Raise your hands as if cheering, then draw a large circle in front of you with both hands.)
We all love our world. (Indicate all the children, then put your hands over your heart.)
w – w – w we, we want peace. (Have the children hold hands.)
Wonderful peace, (Raise your hands as if cheering, but still holding hands.)
We want peace in our world.

📖 Pupil's Book page 88. 3. Listen, point and say.

Draw pupils' attention to activity 3 and say *Point to the picture. w-w-world, w-w-white dove.* Do this two or three times, encouraging pupils to repeat after you. Next, listen to the audio and model how to point to the appropriate picture and say the word.

 64 *w – w – w world. A wonderful world.*
w – w – w white. A white dove.

w – w – w white. A white dove.
w – w – w world. A wonderful world.

👋 Goodbye

Follow the description on page 9.

👋 Extra activities

📖 Teacher Resources Worksheet 31: Draw and colour. Then cut out and stick.

Prepare a worksheet for each pupil in advance and prepare an example showing two children stuck together at the hands, so pupils can see how the activity works. Show pupils your example. Say *Let's draw and colour the children!*

Have pupils draw and colour a face and clothes to personalise their child. After the pupils finish colouring, model how to cut out the child along the dotted lines. Show pupils how to stick the hand of a child to another child's hand to make a line of children.

Teacher Resources Worksheet 32: Trace and colour the world. Then sing the *Phonics World Peace Day* song.

Prepare a worksheet for each pupil in advance and prepare an example world. Have the pupils practise saying the *w* sound in the phrase *Our wonderful world.* Show your example worksheet. Say *This is our world. Our wonderful world! Let's trace and colour the world!*

Play the *Phonics World Peace Day* song (Track 63). Pupils can sing and point to their world.

World Book Day

Lesson objective

To introduce vocabulary related to World Book Day and new phonics sounds ('oa' and 'y').

Language

New: *character, page, story book; boat, goat*
Review: *book, coat, story; brown, green, yellow*
Receptive: *Let's (listen). Show me. Point.*

Materials

Presentation Plus, PB pages 89 and 90, World Book Day Flashcards and downloadable Phonics Flashcards, World Book Day Pop-out, Class Audio, crayons, pencils. Optional: Teacher Resources Worksheets 33 and 34, scissors, glue sticks

🕮 Starting the lesson

Settle the class with an opening routine (see Teacher's Book pages 8 and 9).

🕮 Active time

Warmer

Say *Today is World Book Day. We read stories together and have fun!* Review the colours *green* and *yellow* and teach the vocabulary for World Book Day with the World Book Day Flashcards: *story book, character* and *page*. At this point, you may wish to use the audio of the vocabulary to listen and repeat.

 character, page, story book

🕮 Table time

Say the Table time chant (see page 11).

📖 Pupil's Book page 89. Worksheet 1: Listen, point and say. Then colour.

Help pupils to find the correct page. Hold up your book and point to the different World Book Day vocabulary words in the picture (the story book on the cupboard, the page with writing and Greenman). Say the vocabulary for pupils to repeat after you: *story book, page, character*.

Say *Let's listen!* Play the dialogue once. The children listen and point to the vocabulary items as they hear them. Then play it again, line by line, and have the children repeat each line. Do this until most of the class is participating and saying many of the words. Then play the dialogue several more times, stopping it at various points for children to say the next word.

Direct pupils' attention to the uncoloured pictures. Say *Let's colour the character. What colours? Yes, green and brown!* Demonstrate how to colour Greenman. Repeat with the opposite page, directing pupils to colour it yellow. Let pupils colour the story book on the cupboard however they wish.

Boy:	*It's World Book Day! Look, it's a story book!*
Girl:	*Yes, the teacher reads a story book.*
Boy:	*I can see one, two pages.*
Girl:	*Me, too!*
Girl:	*Oh, look! Look at the character! It's Greenman!*
Boy:	*Yes, I like this character! He's funny!*
Girl:	*Yes, and he's happy. The children are happy, too. They like the character in this story book!*
Boy:	*I like story books!*
Girl:	*Me, too! And I like World Book Day!*

Do the pop-out activity.

Direct pupils' attention to the sample pop-out that you have prepared: a book. Hold up the book and say *Look at the story book!*

Show pupils how to take out the pop-out piece carefully, and how to fold it to make the story book. Observe as they do this and help as needed. Show pupils that three of the pages are blank, and tell them they can draw pictures to create their own story book. Before they start, elicit some ideas for characters and plot, but tell pupils their story can be about anything they like. Point out that a story has a beginning, middle and end, and pupils should draw each of these on the three blank pages.

When all the pupils have finished, say *Show me your story book.* Give pupils time to share their stories with the class.

The pupils can take their story book pop-outs home, or you may wish to hang them in the classroom as part of a World Book Day display.

Extra Phonics Lesson

🔊 Phonics time

📖 **Pupil's Book page 90. 1. Listen and say the *y* and *oa* letter sounds.**

Review previous phonics sounds with the Phonics Flashcards. Review *yellow* and teach *boat* with the World Book Day Phonics Flashcards. Point to the pictures for the sounds in your book and repeat the sounds *y-y-yellow. oa-oa-boat* Play the audio and have pupils listen and repeat three times.

y – y – y	yellow
oa - oa - oa	boat

📖 **Pupil's Book page 90. 2. Sing the song.**

Show pupils the picture in activity 2. Play the song. Point to items in the picture to help pupils understand meaning. After playing the track three times, say it slowly, line by line, and have pupils repeat each line, while looking at the picture. Introduce some gestures for pupils to follow. Play the song again and repeat until pupils are singing at least the *A goat in a coat. Yes! A yellow coat.* parts of the song, and are showing comprehension through gestures.

Open your book, (Put your hands together, then open them like a book.)
Open your book. (Put your hands together, then open them like a book.)
What can you see? (Questioning gesture: palms facing upwards.)
A goat in a coat. (Mime putting on a coat.)
Yes! A yellow coat. (Point to something yellow.)
A goat in a boat. (Move your arms to indicate rowing a boat.)
Yes! A yellow boat. (Point to something yellow.)

📖 **Pupil's Book page 90. 3. Listen, point and say.**

Draw pupils' attention to activity 3 and say *Point to the picture. y-y-yes, y-y-yellow, oa-oa-goat, oa-oa-coat, oa-oa-boat.* Do this two

or three times, encouraging pupils to repeat after you. Next, listen to the audio and model how to point to the appropriate picture and say the word.

y – y – y	yes
y – y – y	yellow
oa - oa - oa	goat
oa - oa - oa	coat
oa - oa - oa	boat
y – y – y	yellow
oa - oa - oa	goat
oa - oa - oa	boat
y – y – y	yes
oa - oa - oa	coat

🔊 Goodbye

Follow the description on page 9.

🔊 Extra activities

Teacher's Resources Worksheet 33: Trace the pages. Draw and colour a character.

Prepare a worksheet for each pupil in advance. Say *Let's trace the pages.* Model how to trace the dashed outline of pages. Once the pupils have finished tracing, ask them *What story book character do you like?* Give an example and elicit some more examples from pupils. Have them draw and colour a character on the book. Make a World Book Day display with the worksheets.

Teacher Resources Worksheet 34: Colour, cut and stick the goat in the boat. Then sing the *Phonics World Book Day* song.

Prepare a worksheet for each pupil in advance and show an example of the goat in a yellow coat sitting in a yellow boat. Have the pupils practise saying the *oa* sound in the words *goat, coat* and *boat*. Show your example goat in a boat. Say *Where's the goat, (Mario)?* Elicit *(In the) boat!* Say *What colour is the boat?* Elicit *Yellow!* Repeat with the coat. Say *Let's colour the goat, the coat and the boat!*

After the pupils finish colouring, model how to cut out the goat and the boat along the dotted lines. Show pupils how to stick the boat over the bottom of the goat, so that it looks like the goat is sitting in the boat. Have the pupils repeat *Look, the goat is in the boat!* as they move their boats along. Play the *Phonics World Book Day* song (Track 68). Pupils can make the boat go up and down in the water for the lines *A goat in a boat. Yes! A yellow boat.*

World Friendship Day

Lesson objective

To introduce vocabulary related to the festival World Friendship Day and a new phonics sound ('ch').

Language

New: *be kind, play games, share; present*
Review: *ball, chair, children, friends, teacher;* colours; numbers; clothes; *A (ball) for you. Thank you.*
Receptive: *Let's (listen). Draw a toy.*

Materials

Presentation Plus, PB pages 91 and 92, World Friendship Day Flashcards and downloadable Phonics Flashcards, World Friendship Day Pop-out, a hand-drawn picture of a ball, Class Audio, crayons, pencils. Optional: Teacher Resources Worksheets 35 and 36, scissors, glue sticks

---

Starting the lesson

Settle the class with an opening routine (see Teacher's Book pages 8 and 9).

Active time

Warmer

Say *Today is World Friendship Day. We play with our friends and we take care of our friends.* Teach vocabulary for World Friendship Day with the World Friendship Day Flashcards: *be kind, play games* and *share*. At this point, you may wish to use the audio of the vocabulary to listen and repeat as a class.

 70 *be kind, play games, share*

Table time

Say the Table time chant (see page 11).

Pupil's Book page 91. Worksheet 1: Listen, point and say. Then colour.

Help pupils to find the correct page. Hold up your book and point to the children representing the different World Friendship Day vocabulary words in the picture. Say the vocabulary for pupils to repeat after you: *be kind, play games, share.*

Say *Let's listen!* Play the dialogue once. The children listen and point to each activity as they hear it. Then play it again, line by line, and have the children repeat each line. Do this until most of

the class is participating and saying many of the words. Then play the dialogue several more times, stopping it at various points for pupils to say the next word.

Say *Let's colour.* Demonstrate how to colour the children. Talk about the different colours pupils have used.

 71

Boy:	*Ooh, look! Children! They're friends.*
Girl:	*Yes, they're friends.*
Boy:	*Look. Share. They're sharing the book.*
Girl:	*Oh, yes. I share! I share books with my friends.*
Boy:	*Me, too!*
Girl:	*Oh, dear. Look at the girl. She's sad.*
Boy:	*Yes, she's sad. But her friend is kind. It's good to be kind.*
Girl:	*Yes. I'm kind to my friends.*
Boy:	*I'm kind to my friends, too.*
Girl:	*Look! Play games. Friends play games together.*
Boy:	*Yes! I play games with my friends.*
Girl:	*It's World Friendship Day, so …*
Both:	*Let's play a game with our friends!*

Do the pop-out activity.

Direct pupils' attention to the sample pop-out that you have prepared: a present, with a picture of a ball that you drew, inside it. Hold up the present and say *Look at the present! What is it?* Have pupils guess what might be in the present. Open it, and say *Look! It's a ball. A ball for my friend.* Give the ball to a pupil and say *A ball for you.* Have the pupils pass the ball round, saying *A ball for you!* and *Thank you.*

Show pupils how to take out the pop-out piece carefully, and how to fold it in half to make a present. Observe as they do this and help as needed.

Give each pupil a piece of paper. Say *Draw a toy for a friend* and have them draw something they think a friend would like to receive as a present, and put it inside the present.

When all the pupils have finished, have the pupils sit in a circle, and give their present to the child next to them. Encourage them to say *A present for you!* as they give the present, and *Thank you!* when they receive one.

Extra Phonics Lesson

🔖 Phonics time

📖 Pupil's Book page 92. 1. Listen and say the *ch* letter sound.

Review previous phonics sounds with the Phonics Flashcards. Review *chair* with the World Friendship Day Phonics Flashcard. Point to the picture for the sound in your book and repeat the sound as you point *ch-ch-chair* Play the audio and have pupils listen and repeat three times.

72 ch – ch   chair

📖 Pupil's Book page 92. 2. Sing the song.

Show pupils the picture in activity 2. You may wish to explain (in L1) that the children in the picture are playing a game of *Musical chairs*. They dance to some music, around the chairs. The teacher takes away one chair. When the teacher stops the music, everyone rushes to sit on a chair. Any child who doesn't have a chair is out of the game. Play continues until there is one child left sitting on a chair. Ask pupils if they have played a game like *Musical chairs* before.

Play the song. Point to items in the picture to help pupils understand meaning. After playing the track three times, say it slowly, line by line, and have pupils repeat each line, while looking at the picture. Introduce some gestures for pupils to follow. Play the song again and repeat until pupils are singing at least the *Children, play a game with your friends* part of the song, and are showing comprehension through gestures.

73 Ch - ch children, (Point to the children.)
Ch - ch chairs, (Point to the chairs.)
Ch - ch children, (Point to the children.)
Ch - ch chairs. (Point to the chairs.)
Children, (Point to the children.)
play a game with your friends. (Hold both hands with a partner, and dance round in a circle together.)
Sit on your chair (Point to a chair.)
when the music ends! (Wait till the end of the song, then sit down.)

📖 Pupil's Book page 92. 3. Listen and circle *ch*. Listen, point and say.

Draw pupils' attention to activity 3. First, point to each picture and say the words for pupils to repeat, emphasising the *ch* sound. Then point to the written words and have pupils identify *ch* in each word. Have pupils notice that the *ch* in *teacher* is in the middle of the word. Say *Listen and circle 'ch'.* Play the first part of the audio and pause for pupils to circle the letters. Monitor as they work. Then say *Now, let's listen and point.* Play the second part of the audio, pausing after each sound for pupils to point and repeat.

74 ch - ch - ch   chair
ch - ch - ch   children
ch - ch - ch   teacher

ch - ch - ch   children
ch - ch - ch   teacher
ch - ch - ch   chair

🍃 Goodbye

Follow the description on page 9.

🍃 Extra activities

Teacher Resources Worksheet 35: Draw yourself. Then colour the friends.

Prepare a worksheet for each pupil in advance. Say *They're friends.* Model how to draw your own face and hair on the middle child. Once the pupils have finished drawing, ask them to colour the clothes on the three friends, the ball and the game. Have pupils talk about the colours and clothes the friends are wearing. Make a World Friendship Day display with the worksheets.

Teacher Resources Worksheet 36: Colour, cut and stick the child and the chair. Then sing the *Phonics World Friendship Day* song.

Prepare a worksheet for each pupil in advance and show an example finger puppet child. Have the pupils practise saying the *ch* sound in the words *child* and *chair*. Show your example finger puppet and move it on and off the chair. Say *Where's the child, (Luis)?* Elicit *On the chair!* Say *Let's colour the child and the chair!*

After the pupils finish colouring, model how to cut out the child and the chair along the dotted lines. Show pupils how to stick the front and back of the child together to make a finger puppet. Repeat *Look, the child is on the chair!* Have the pupils put on their finger puppets. Explain they are going to play *Musical chairs* with their puppets. Play the *Phonics World Friendship Day* song (Track 73). Pupils can make their child play with other child puppets (so there is a group of children), then sit on the chair at the end, when they hear the line *Sit on your chair when the music ends.*

Green Day

Lesson objective

To introduce vocabulary related to Easter and a new phonics sound ('ai/ay').

Language

New: *help, park, rubbish*
Review: *forest, snake, train; clean up, play; rainy; colours*
Receptive: *Let's (fold). Put our birds in the tree. Point.*

Materials

Presentation Plus, PB pages 93 and 94, Green Day Flashcards and downloadable Phonics Flashcards, Green Day Pop-outs, Class Audio, crayons, pencils. Optional: Teacher Resources Worksheets 37 and 38, scissors

🍃 Starting the lesson

Settle the class with an opening routine (see Teacher's Book pages 8 and 9).

🍃 Active time

Warmer

Say *Today is Green Day! We tidy up and take care of the forest!* Present Green Day vocabulary with the Green Day Flashcards: *help, park* and *rubbish*. At this point, you may wish to use the audio of the vocabulary to listen and repeat as a class.

 75 help, park, rubbish

Let's clean up song

Say *Let's sing a 'Green Day' song! Let's listen!* Play the song once and do the actions. Then have the pupils stand up and sing the song line by line while doing the actions. Play the song several times for practice.

 76 **Let's clean up**

Let's clean up and help each other (Pretend to pick things up from the floor.)

*To keep the **forest** clean.* (Put your palms together above your head to make the shape of a treetop.)

Let's clean up and help each other (As above.)

*To keep the **forest** green.* (As above.)

Please be careful, tidy up! (Hands together as if pleading.)

Don't drop rubbish, pick it up! (Shake your finger 'no', pretend to pick something up.)

Let's clean up and help each other (As above.)

*To keep the **forest** clean.* (As above.)

Repeat with:
park (Pretend your hand is a slide.)

🍃 Table time

Say the Table time chant (see page 11).

Do the pop-out activity.

Direct pupils' attention to the sample pop-out that you have prepared: a tree card and a bird. Hold up your example pop-out, show the bird peeking out from inside the tree and say *Now, I can see the bird.* Then put your bird inside the tree card and say *Now I can't see the bird. He is hidden in the tree.*

Show pupils how to take out the pop-out pieces carefully. Observe as they do this and help as needed.

Say *Let's fold our tree to make a card.* Model how to carefully fold the tree in half. Once the class have their trees ready, say *Let's put our birds in the tree.* Model how to place the bird in the tree. You can choose to glue the birds inside, or not.

 Pupil's Book page 93. Worksheet 1. Colour and trace.

Help pupils to find the correct page. Say the vocabulary words and point to the pictures in your own book *park, rubbish, help.* Say *Let's trace the lines.* Point to the lines on the fence for the pupils to trace. Point out the 'Park' sign, the rubbish bag and boy carrying the bag. Say *Let's finish colouring!*

Extra Phonics Lesson

 **Phonics time**

 Pupil's Book page 94. 1. Listen and say the *ai/ay* letter sound.

Review previous phonics sounds with the Phonics Flashcards. Introduce *rainy day* with the Green Day Phonics Flashcard. Repeat the words stretching them out for the pupils to repeat *rai-ai-ainy, day-ay-ay.* Point to the picture for the sound in your book. Play the audio and have pupils listen and repeat three times.

> **77**
> ai - ai - ai   rain   rainy
> ay - ay - ay   day   rainy day

 Pupil's Book page 94. 2. Sing the song.

Play the song. Use gestures to help pupils understand meaning. After playing the track three times, say it slowly, line by line, and have pupils repeat each line (following your lead to use gestures where possible). Continue to repeat until pupils are saying at least the *ay, ay, ay. It's a beautiful day* parts.

> **78**
> *ay - ay - ay* (Arms outstretched above head with hands together.)
>
> *It's a beautiful day!* (Open hands wide and look up, as if at the sky.)
>
> *Let's go out,* (Walking motion.)
>
> *And play, play, play!* (Dance on the spot.)
>
> *ay - ay - ay* (Arms outstretched above head with hands together.)
>
> *It's a beautiful day!* (Open hands wide and look up, as if at the sky.)
>
> *Let's go out,* (Walking motion.)

> *And play in the rain!* (Rain falling gesture with fingertips.)
>
> *What do you say, say, say,* (Questioning gesture: palms facing upwards.)
>
> *On this beautiful day?* (Open hands wide and look up, as if at the sky.)
>
> *ay - ay - ay* (Arms outstretched above head with hands together.)
>
> *It's a beautiful day!* (Open hands wide and look up, as if at the sky.)

 Pupil's Book page 94. 3. Listen and match. Listen, point and say.

Write the following words on the board and draw a picture above each one: *play, snake, train, rain.* Point first to the picture and say the word, then the written word and have pupils repeat the word. Direct pupils' attention to activity 3. Say *Point to the picture. Sna-a-ke, rai-ai-ain, pla-a-ay, trai-ai-ain.* Do this two or three times. Then play the audio and pause after each word. Model how to connect the picture to the correct word. Point to the pictures and words on the board to help. Play the audio again, pausing after each sound and word for pupils to point and repeat.

> **79**
> snake, rain, play, train

Goodbye

Follow the description on page 9.

Extra activities

Teacher Resources Worksheet 37: Help Sam and Nico recycle the rubbish.

Prepare a worksheet for each pupil in advance. Say *Oh no! Sam and Nico need to put the rubbish in the bin. Follow the trail.* Model tracing a trail with your finger. Say *Use your crayon to get Sam and Nico to the bin.* Have pupils follow the dashed line. As they get to a piece of rubbish, they can colour it. Monitor as pupils work and help as needed.

Teacher Resources Worksheet 38: Make a rainy day puzzle. Then sing the *Phonics Green Day* song.

Prepare a worksheet for each pupil in advance. Also prepare a completed puzzle as an example. You may want to practise vocabulary by saying *What's this?* Emphasise the *ai* in rainy and rainbow and the *ay* in day. Have pupils colour the picture, then cut along the dotted lines to make their puzzle pieces. Once the children have their pieces, they can swap their puzzles with a partner and complete each other's rainy day puzzle.

Summer fun!

Lesson objective
To review summer vocabulary and learn a song about summer.

Language
New: *beach, cool, holiday, swim*
Review: *blue, orange, yellow; hot, sunny; play;* course vocabulary
Receptive: *Point to the (beach). Do we need a (bucket)?*

Materials
Presentation Plus, Greenman Puppet, PB page 95, Flashcards Units 1–6, Class Audio, pictures of people on a summer holiday, crayons, pencils. Optional: PB page 96, Teacher Resources Worksheets 39–40, paints, scissors, glue sticks, Level A End-of-year certificate for each pupil

🐛 Starting the lesson

Settle the class with an opening routine (see Teacher's Book pages 8 and 9).

🐛 Active time

Warmer

Review weather vocabulary (you can use the Routine Boards on Presentation Plus to do this). Pupils can choose the vocabulary that is most appropriate for summer. Have the pupils use gestures to show the different types of weather (make a big sun over your head with your arms for *sunny*, fan yourself for *hot*). Ask *What's the weather like today? Is it sunny? Is it cold? Is it rainy? Is it summer?*

Say the vocabulary.

Have Greenman hold up flashcards for some of the course vocabulary, including the vocabulary shown on page 95 of the Pupil's Book (*window, sandpit, bucket, spade, coat, hat, sheep* and *juice*). Have the pupils say (or repeat) each word. Then, speed up to get the children to identify the words as quickly as possible.

Happy summer holiday! song

Show some pictures of people on a summer holiday, e.g. sitting on a beach, and present the words *holiday* and *beach*. Then say *It's a summer holiday, let's go to the beach!* Model putting on sunglasses and suncream and sunbathing, for pupils to copy. Say *It's very hot! Let's swim!* Model swimming in place and have the pupils join in. Say *Again! Oh, it's very hot! Let's swim!* Monitor to make sure the pupils recognise the words and do the gestures

without you modelling them. Then say *Ahh, the water is cool.* and encourage pupils to repeat.

Play the song once and model the actions. Then have the pupils join in as you say the song line by line and do the actions with them. Repeat this until most pupils are saying some of the words and participating in the actions. Then play the audio again, modelling the actions with the pupils participating. Repeat the song until the class is singing most of the words and doing the actions.

 Happy summer holiday! 🎵

The sun is hot and orange today. (Hold your hands over your head with fingertips from your hands touching to make a big 'sun'.)

The water is cool and blue, hooray! (Make waves with your hands, then raise one arm for 'hooray'.)

We can swim and play all day. (Pretend to swim in place.)

Happy summer holiday! (Stretch your hands up and out as if making a big announcement.)

The sun is hot and yellow today. (Hold your hands over your head with fingertips from your hands touching to make a big 'sun'.)

The water is cool and blue, hooray! (Make waves with your hands, then raise one arm for 'hooray'.)

We can swim and play all day.
(Pretend to swim in place.)

Happy summer holiday! (Stretch your hands up
and out as if making a big announcement.)

🖐 Table time

Say the Table time chant (see page 11).

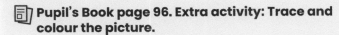 Pupil's Book page 95. Worksheet 1: Circle the beach items and say.

Show pupils page 95 and walk around to check that everyone
is on the correct page. Say *Point to the pictures.* Say each of the
vocabulary words: *window, spade, bucket, sandpit, coat, juice,
sheep, hat.* Now say *Point to the beach. There it is! It is hot! What
do we need? Do we need a window? No. Do we need a bucket?
Yes.* Trace around the example circle with your finger. Continue
the process with one or two more items and then let pupils work
independently to draw a circle around the beach items, as you
monitor their work. When you check answers, encourage pupils
to give reasons for their answers in L1, e.g. *Juice is a beach item
because you get thirsty when it's hot. A winter hat is not a beach
item because it's for cold weather.* You may want to point out that
a summer hat would be very useful for a day at the beach. Pupils
may circle the spade, the sandpit and the juice.

Have pupils point to each item again and say the word.

🖐 Goodbye

Follow the description on page 9.

🖐 Extra activities

🖐 Pupil's Book page 96. Extra activity: Trace and colour the picture.

Show pupils page 96 in your book and check to be sure they
are all on the right page. Say *Look at the shape of the pool.
Make the lines of the pool in the air.* Model how to do this.
Say *What shape is the pool? (A rectangle.)* Repeat with the
ring. Now, hold up your book to show how to trace the lines
of the pool, Greenman's umbrella and the floating ring. Say
Let's trace the lines and colour. Pupils should be able to work
independently on this. Monitor as they work.

Teacher Resources Worksheets 39 and 40: Paint, cut and stick to make a swimming pool scene.

Prepare the summer project worksheets for each pupil in
advance. Play the song: *Happy summer holiday!* (Track 80)
again. Hold up Worksheet 39 and say *Look, it's a swimming
pool! Let's paint!* Model painting the swimming pool. When
pupils have finished, hold up Worksheet 40 and say *Who's
that?* (point to Greenman) and elicit *Greenman* from the
pupils. Repeat until the pupils have named each character.
Have them paint or colour the characters. When the pupils
have finished colouring/painting, model cutting out the
characters. Say *Let's put Greenman in the swimming
pool!* Model sticking Greenman onto the pool. Repeat with
the other characters. Make a summer display with the
worksheets.

Greenman and the Magic Forest Level A End-of-year certificate

Print out a certificate for each pupil. Fill in their name and,
if you wish, a special congratulatory message. Invite one
pupil at a time to the front of the class and give them their
diploma or have Greenman do this. Say *Congratulations!*
After all the pupils have received their certificates, play
some of their favourite songs from the course and let
them celebrate.